The Other Side of the Door

The Other Side of the Door

A How to Guide for Connecting with Loved Ones Who Have Crossed Over

PATRICIA FERO

ISBN: 1530905869
ISBN 13: 9781530905867

Dedication

To my sister, Nene, who greeted me at the threshold of Heaven.
You have enriched my life beyond measure.

Gone From My Sight

I am standing by the seashore.
A ship at my side spreads her white sails to the morning breeze
And starts for the blue ocean.
She is an object of beauty and strength
And I stand and watch
Until at last she hangs like a speck of white cloud
Just where the sun and sky come down to mingle with each other.
Then someone at my side says
"There she goes."
Gone where? Gone from my sight-that is all.

She is just as large in mast and hull and span.
As she was when she left my side
And just as able to bear her load of liv-
ing freight to the port of destination.
Her diminished size is in me, not in her.

And just at the moment when someone at my side says
"There she goes."
There are other eyes watching her coming
And other voices ready to take up the glad shout,
"Here she comes."
And that is dying

Henry Van Dyke

T his is a poem that I came across in the back of a little Hospice pamphlet given to the family as Nene was nearing the end of her life. This was an early inspiration, for me, in my early stages of opening to life after death.

Table of Contents

Acknowledgements

L inda Stoker is the first name that comes to me as I reflect on the process of writing this book. Linda took my illegible writings from the very beginning and converted them into neat, orderly early pages of this project. Slowly, with significant effort, finally, this completed book emerged. She persistently assisted me through this process with patience and generosity of spirit.

Lauri Keller was able to move into the spirit of the book so readily and supported me with her ongoing ability to tune into spirit. Her vision for the cover was the inspiration for the beautiful artwork done by my son, artist, Tony Fero. He created the cover image as well as the whimsical frame for the quotes that are sprinkled throughout the book.

Friend and artist Linda Robinson did the little crow at the base of the door. The sweet crow with the tiara and the milkweed seed in her month was inspired by her perception of Nene's playful nature.

Victoria Hanchin plays such an enormous part in my life by being my "goddess soul sister." There is no way to describe her support in the completion of my "divine assignments."

Krysten Wall has been such a mentor to me in trusting and inhabiting the world of spirit. The unseen realms are territories she travels in comfortably and has supported me in gaining so much comfort with this experience.

I am grateful to Cezar Valdez for his skilled personal training in IADC (induced after death communication). Wendy Taylor edited the book with the heart and passion of someone who is engaged with her own ongoing communication with a loved one on the other side of the door.

I am grateful to Terri Lewis for her interest and belief from the beginning. Her husband, Sam, and Nene used to argue about who would get to heaven first and if God would be a man or a woman. Nene left shortly after Sam. Hopefully, they are in agreement now.

Kathy Perry was such a powerful support in our daily walks with our dogs, Nocho and Dexter. She asked for regular reports on my progress. This played an important role in my staying motivated.

Mona and Ken Hitchcock played such an important role in encouraging me from the beginning. Ken has shown me the best I have ever witnessed in a supportive and loving husband to Mona. Mona has provided profound catalytic energy for me as part of my ongoing motivation to complete this book. My intention is to inspire her to tell her extraordinary story of love for and from her mother who now resides on the "other side of the door."

I thank Jean Shinoda Bolen for being Jean Shinoda Bolen. I am one of the millions who have been inspired and positively impacted by her work.

I am eternally grateful to Gretchen and Liza for being my lifetime friends. I don't know what I would do without either of you.

Last and she knows she's not least, Tama Kieves who continues to keep me inspired and believing that I am so much more than I think I am. I once heard that we should see ourselves the way our dog sees us. Tama sees me with as much excitement, joy, and loyalty as my dog Dexter. Thank you Tama for being my coach and fellow lover of *The Course in Miracles*.

"And life is eternal and love immortal, and death is only a horizon, and a horizon is nothing save the limit of our sight."

Rudolph Steiner

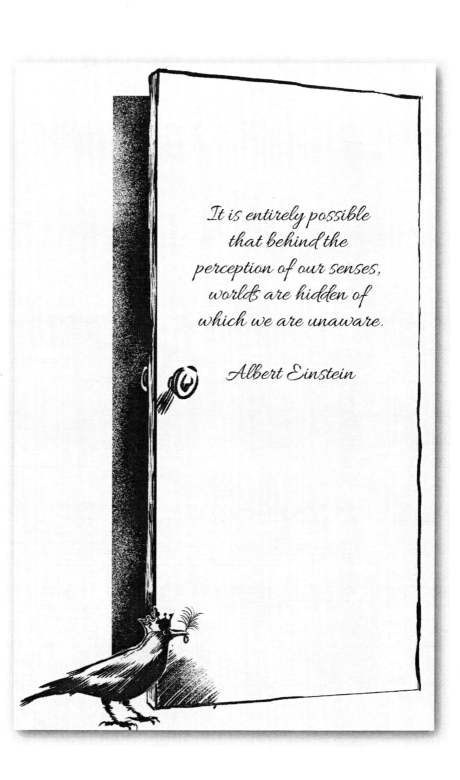

*It is entirely possible
that behind the
perception of our senses,
worlds are hidden of
which we are unaware.*

Albert Einstein

DOUBT

Writing a book like this is not without trepidation. We live in a world that gives credence to what can be proven, and questions what cannot. I am a psychotherapist. My livelihood depends on my being credible, stable and sane.

What happens to my reputation if I write a book about connecting with loved ones who have "crossed over" (died). Words like flaky, crazy, weirdo are frequently ascribed to people who talk about these things, let alone write about them in black and white and sign their name to be preserved forever. You cannot really take it back once you publish it.

This morning, as I was struggling with these doubts, two things happened. First, I received an email from my dear friend Victoria Hanchin announcing a recently released book by a favorite author and promoter named Arielle Ford. The book is titled *Love on the Other Side.*

Later that morning I was walking my dog, Dexter, and a friend stopped me to announce that she heard several loud caws from a crow and then the song titled "Denise, Denise" popped into her mind. A special section of the book is devoted to my experience with Nene and crows. The chorus of the song is "Denise, Denise. I'm so in love with you." I have learned that connecting with my feelings of love toward her—between us—opens the channel for our communication.

As I continued with my doubt and talked to Nene, as I often did with my questions, she suggested Googling books in After Death Communication. Not only are there hundreds, maybe thousands of books and articles, I also found sites combining science and spirituality attempting to reconcile these two seemingly separate worlds.

My concerns about sounding crazy, weird, flaky began to diminish significantly. I was certainly in good company. Elizabeth Kubler-Ross, Raymond Moody, Eben Alexander, Astronaut Edgar Mitchell, Rudolf Steiner, and The Dali Lama were all on the long list of those who believe we can connect with those in the afterlife.

Now I was beginning to see myself in the company of people I admired and not someone whose credibility would be questioned. Maybe it would be, but now I was prepared and less afraid of this; so much for the doubt. I am now ready to move forward on a project that was strongly prompted by my spirit. I could not prove my spirit, but I sure knew it was real.

Working through my doubt is an ongoing process. If you, the reader, choose to open to connecting with your loved ones, I suspect doubt will be part of your process as well. I hope my experiences will be helpful to you.

About Nene

Who Is Nenie Beanie?

Nenie Beanie is Pat's sister who left her body at 11:11am Friday, August 13, 2004. She spent the last 14 years of her life on earth deepening her spiritual path through the experience of living with 4th stage metatisized breast cancer. Nene used her immenent death as a catalyst for her spiritual growth.

Her last words before she died were, "The Circle of Love is Never Broken." This began to be demonstrated when she began communicating to Pat 3 days after she transitioned. She and Pat have continued to connect through channeled writing for the last 12 years.

Nene's Story

When my sister, Nene, died of breast cancer on August 13, 2004, little did I know that her story and my relationship with her would continue as a central theme for the rest of my life.

Nene began communicating with me three days after she left this world and is present with me as I write these words. Her entry into my life as her spirit began in a compelling way.

I was driving to work and stopped at a stop sign waiting for a car to pass. The car was moving a little slowly and drove into the lane I was waiting to pull into. As the car passed, I saw that it was another sister, Cathy, who did not live in this area. We missed recognizing one another until she had passed and I thought to myself, "That was close." I continued driving the block to my office and started to enter the building only to have to back up as someone came out of the door I was opening. Another near miss. I proceeded up the stairs to the door that opened into the suite of offices I worked in and as I began to turn the doorknob, it turned from the other side and someone exited. At this point, I think I mumbled out loud to myself, "What is going on with doors?" I began my session with my client, moving myself into a receptive state. As I listened to her, a voice in my head said with crystal clarity, "I'm just on the other side of the door." I glanced at the clock. It was 11:11 AM. I knew it was Nene.

And so it began. I started writing to her on an almost daily basis for the better part of 11 years. I am not as disciplined about writing everyday as I was, but my communication is ongoing and powerful. Our relationship has continued and deepened since she left her body and is the reason I am now, finally, writing this book.

My intention in doing this is to offer hope and information to support others in knowing that our love and connection continues after death and that we can learn how to develop and grow that bond of love and understanding and receptivity as long as we choose to do so, and our loved one chooses this as well.

I have lived this and am living it now as I am writing these words. As I wrote the last sentence, Nene insisted that I include the word receptivity in the description. I suspect that we will learn more as we go along. My experience has taught me to listen carefully and to trust these promptings from her. This is not just my story, but it's Nene's story, as well. After all, we are writing it together.

"We came from love. We forgot we were love. We are returning to love."
Nenie Beanie

Love is power.
Let it be.
Let it roar.

Nenie Beanie

A Family Comes Together

After her breast cancer diagnosis, Nene managed with significant struggle to continue to care for her children; maintain a household as a single parent; and even work for several years. Her fourth stage cancer diagnosis had been when the twins were six months old. Now they were 10 and everything seemed to come crashing in at once. Her financial situation continued to worsen until she ultimately was unable to maintain her house. Her health was deteriorating along with the rest of her life. Her house was being foreclosed on and she had nowhere to live and take care of her children

Her life had exploded. Nene's ability to manage her life was completely gone. A profound series of events was set into motion that manifested in the, as yet inconceivable, but ultimately miraculous solution to what was an impossible situation. How would she and the twins go on?

The first thing that happened was that she called me and told me that she was losing her house. I was reading *The Course in Miracles*, as I received her call and my immediate and inspired response was, "You can move in with me."

My sister, Barb, had been playing a highly active role in helping care for her twins. Barb also had a 10-year-old son and the cousins were more like siblings. It was a natural choice tor the twins to stay with Barb who lived less than a mile away. Nene could rest at my house most of the time and could spend time with her children at Barb's when she had enough energy to be out of bed and with them.

In the meantime, our sister, Cathy, who lived in Washington D.C., was reeling from the 9-11 attack as Washington was preparing for possible future terrorist outbreaks. Cathy worked for a hospital system, which was immersed in preparing for possible future occurrences. She decided this might be a good time to return to Michigan and be closer to family. She made the decision; came to Michigan; sold her condo in Alexandra; and purchased a beautiful lake home with a fully equipped lower level apartment in less than a month.

These arrangements set the stage for family members working together like a well-oiled machine for the final four years of Nene's life.

Barb was a full-time, working, single mother of her 10-year-old son when she took the role of second mother for Nene's 10-year-old twins, Robert and Katlyn. Now, she was a single mom with three 10-year old children. She rose to the occasion with amazing competence and love. She was, however, a human being and was exhausted much of the time. This is where Cathy's amazing move comes in.

Cathy took the role of supportive aunt most seriously. She created a haven in her new home for rest and replenishment for everyone. She had plenty of living and sleeping rooms for both Nene and her children in the downstairs apartment. They all stayed every weekend at her house while Barb got some badly needed rest. Nene was sleeping many hours a day and was only able to be up and functional a few hours a day. The rest of the time, she required sleep. During this time, Cathy was entertaining the kids; cooking for everyone and setting the stage for Nene to be up and playing cards and board games with her children. This gave everyone an opportunity for quality time to connect and enjoy one another.

When Nene was first diagnosed, her plan was for Cathy and her husband to take her children when she died. Barb and Cathy were very close, and they both worked hard to support Cathy and her husband's relationship with Kate and Robert over the distance from D.C. to Michigan. They spent holidays together and planned at least one vacation together each summer.

When Cathy moved to Michigan and made a nurturing space for Nene and her children, it was as if the twins had three mothers, Cathy, Barb and Nene. Over the years as Barb spent most of the time caring for them, she transitioned into the primary maternal role after Nene died when the twins were 14.

As the book was almost ready to go to print, I gave my mother a copy of the manuscript to look over. She reminded me that I had left out the fact that Nene and I had a conflict within the last year of her life. I asked her to leave my home and she went to live with Mom and Dad and remained there until she died.

I was reticent about adding this information as the book was completed. Upon reflection, I felt guided to include it, as the message is important. My goal was to paint a beautiful picture of the cooperation of the family in supporting Nene in her illness and prolonged dying process.

Mom's injunction to "make sure it is authentic," is a point well-made and worthy of "stopping the presses," to be included. My guilt about asking Nene to leave is also a part of my ongoing connection with her and part of my flawed humanity.

This most likely is something we all have to deal with, as we all have complicated relationships with loved ones.

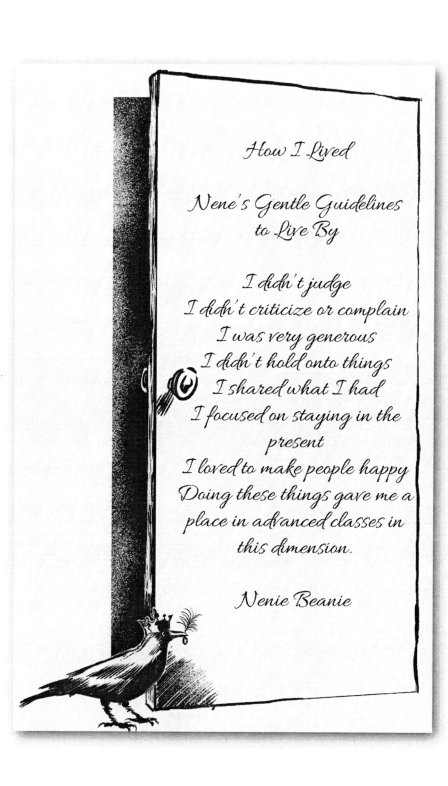

How I Lived

Nene's Gentle Guidelines
to Live By

I didn't judge
I didn't criticize or complain
I was very generous
I didn't hold onto things
I shared what I had
I focused on staying in the
present
I loved to make people happy
Doing these things gave me a
place in advanced classes in
this dimension.

Nenie Beanie

Nene's Story from Her Perspective

This writing was done by Nene before she died. I stumbled across it in a box of her writings when we cleaned out her house. This is one of her many writings.

My journey intensified for me about eight years ago. At the time I was so involved with the trappings of the world that I didn't recognize what I now see as "God's thump on the head", trying to awaken me out of a downward spiraling dream world.

I would wake up in the middle of the night at least five times a week in a terrified state; sweat would be covering my entire body, and I would be gasping for air. I was absolutely convinced that if I went back to sleep I would never wake up again. I would sit there and try to override the terror by talking to myself from a "rational" place. I sought answers from experts, and the answer I was given was "panic attacks brought on by stress." That seemed reasonable enough. My life at the time was certainly stressful.

I was a single mother working two jobs to make ends meet. My schedule at the time allowed me approximately two to three hours of sleep a night, seven days a week for a two-to- three-week stretch with one day off between stretches. This pattern continued for one and a half years nonstop, with the additional complication that I was battling alcoholism.

Eventually the message, which I now believe was God's message, became more clearly defined. I was diagnosed with cancer. At the point of my diagnosis, the disease had already spread from its origin in my breast through the lymph system and into several points in my bones. The prognosis was not particularly promising.

My surgeon informed me that I had already had the disease for six to eight years, and my oncologist told me that without treatment I would be dead in six months to a year. Even with treatment, there were no guarantees how long I could survive. There was nothing that could cure the disease at this stage of progression.

Well, needless to say, my life was in turmoil. I was confused and very frightened for myself and for my children. My particular method of coping was to minimize the situation outwardly to the people around me and in retrospect to myself, as well. As it turned out, it seemed to be an effective battle plan because my physical progress seemed to surprise my family and my doctors.

While my attitude to the outside world was, "Aw shucks! No big deal… it's under control," and I improved somewhat, inside a pressure was building. I went through a depression and ironically for a person with a terminal disease, suicidal feelings. I did some individual therapy, and finally joined a group where I met with a woman who was to be my guide as I sought to reclaim my life, a journey I continue to this day. *(This was written in the late 90's. Nene died in 2004.)*

My new friend and I began to notice quickly that we had a multitude of things in common. At the time, I found each of these discoveries the most amazing coincidences. I know now that these were waiting for the right time to offer resources.

Now I know, too, that no one accepts insight until they are ready. We are each at different points of spiritual readiness. Trying to accelerate a spiritual process can actually have a reactive and delaying effect. I also learned with my friend that we are all teachers and students simultaneously; for these two seemingly opposite roles are, in fact, an exchange and cannot be separated.

The people that seem to cross our paths haphazardly are opportunities to teach and learn.

When I awakened to the seriousness of my condition, I made a request to God. I asked God to allow me to stay here only if I would be the best person to raise my children. If they would be better off with my sister and brother-in-law, then I was ready for Him to take me. I asked for the strength to cope with whatever decision He made.

After years of searching, I have finally understood the wisdom and the folly of that request. The folly was my own self-importance. The wisdom lies in the acceptance. I could have just as easily said, "Thy will be done."

Our Connection

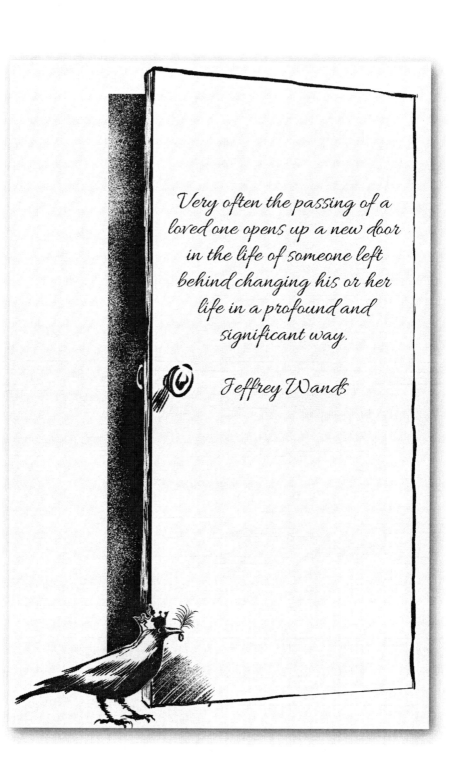

Very often the passing of a loved one opens up a new door in the life of someone left behind changing his or her life in a profound and significant way.

Jeffrey Wands

An Invitation

I experienced my sister Nene's voice three days after she died saying, "I'm just on the other side of the door." I thought at first that it was an announcement; she was telling me she was still here. I was so grateful for the message that I immediately started communicating with her after that.

Now, more than 10 years later and thousands of hours of written communication, I begin this book with the discovery that the long-ago invitation was intended to maintain my relationship with my sister. I did so and the rewards have been immeasurable.

I am going to list a few as examples to illustrate the treasures that I, and many others, have received as a result of the lines of communication being kept open after a loved one's transition. I have learned that this is true for all of us as we keep the connection open. Those who have crossed over have so many gifts to offer all of us if only we attend to and listen to what they have to say. Following are a few examples of gifts Nene has given:

1. A beautiful set of meditation cards inspired by her words of wisdom. These cards have positively impacted hundreds of people. Many say they can feel the connection with her when they use the cards. They have offered comfort and insight on countless occasions. The cards are called "Seeds from My Sister."

2. My ongoing communication with Nene has deepened my spiritual walk. As I write to her and listen internally for her response, I have honed my capacities for inner listening to an extraordinary level. My communication with the unseen world has increased dramatically. My relationship with the Holy Spirit has been deepened by my ability to "Listen fiercely."

3. I have given workshops and retreats providing knowledge about how to connect with those who have crossed over. They have been profound and valuable to the people who attended.

4. The inspiration and prompting to write this book is obviously a result of my well-established communication with Nene. I believe we are at a point in our spiritual evolution that the floodgates between the material world and the world of spirit have opened. Those who have crossed over have so much to offer and help us in this transition. As others are inspired to do this by reading this book, infinite resources can come through to assist us all.

These are only a few examples of how my communication with Nene after she crossed over has affected not only me but also others on the material plane. I never could have had the slightest clue of all that was to transpire after I chose to respond to what I thought was an announcement, but now feel secure in the newfound knowledge that it was an 'invitation.' I am so glad I accepted this invitation. It's been quite a party!

"We're meant to engage in all kinds of things on earth – things that don't make sense from a human point of view. So take a moment before you judge your fellow man too harshly. A lot of people judged me, but I was dealing with circumstances I had signed up to explore before I was born."

Annie Kagan
The Afterlife of Billy Fingers

From subtle whispers to psychic screams they're constantly doing whatever they think is necessary to connect with one another and with our own life's purpose.

Jeffrey Wands

Ms. Right

*M*y sister, Nene, LOVED to be right. She was famous for her relentless pursuit of proving herself right on one topic or another; the verbal jousting went on forever once she got her teeth into a subject. She never quit until she had proven she was right. This made for countless lively and sometimes loud conversations,

Several years ago when I was in the early stages of communicating with her (I always did it through writing.) I noticed that I misspelled words in unexpected ways. I have always been an excellent speller and these misspellings began attracting my attention because they were so unusual and frequent.

As I began to pay more attention and flowed with them, I began discovering that Nene caused me to misspell a word when she wanted me to pay attention to some information in particular. I tuned into this pattern and had a dialogue with her about this. She humorously informed me that these miswrites were because she was "Ms. Right." This gave me a huge, incredulous laugh and helped me in my awareness that whenever these misspellings popped up they were from "Ms. Right," and she had something she wanted me to pay attention to so I would delve further into whatever topic we were communicating about.

During the writing of this piece, I experienced five misspellings and one whole phrase written incorrectly. So, as you read this, you can know that what I have just written was virtually channeled by "Ms. Right."

This is a unique way of deepening communication between Nene and me. As you become more practiced and skilled with communication with your loved ones, you may also receive special ways of knowing that this connection is very real and worthy of being trusted.

"*This is what it comes down to: That we learn to experience that those who have passed through the gate of death have only assumed another form. Having died, they stand before our feelings like those who, through life experiences, have traveled to distant lands, whither we can follow them only later. We have, therefore, nothing to bear but a time of separation.*"

Rudolph Steiner

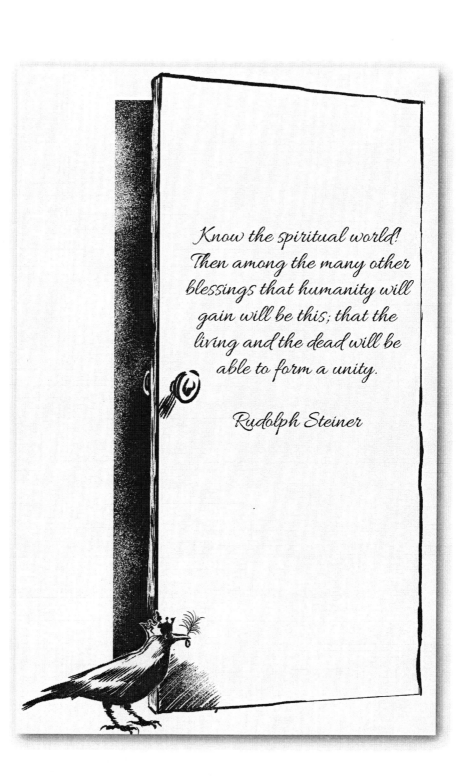

Know the spiritual world!
Then among the many other
blessings that humanity will
gain will be this; that the
living and the dead will be
able to form a unity.

Rudolph Steiner

Working in Tandem

*M*y communication with Nene began three days after she transitioned and continues to this day 11 years later. In writing to her this morning, what came through is that our relationship can be a model for others who want to maintain their own connection with their loved ones who have crossed over.

It was certainly unexpected to me when I first heard her announce, "I'm just on the other side of the door." It continued to be unpredictable, but most often with such surprising gifts. The creation of the resulted in a magical summer "Seeds from My Sister" cards of putting them together and countless testimonials of their impact on those who used them. Many said they could feel Nene's presence as they worked with the cards.

This is such a powerful example of how my resources in human form could be used in harmony with Nene's spirit in the creation of a tool that assisted many people in accessing more of their spiritual selves. This is a concrete example of "bringing spirit into matter." Nene and I are just two individuals; her in spirit and me in human form demonstrating just a small example of working in tandem from both sides of the veil.

As each of you read this book and most likely have someone, in particular, in mind that you want to connect with, this opportunity is waiting for you. What an incredible win/win situation. You can access your connection with your loved one and you can decide together what kinds of gifts you want to offer the world together as a result of your communication and connection.

This is a time when the veil between heaven and earth is thinning. Taking advantage of this unprecedented opportunity to bring love onto the earth in partnership with your loved is yours for the choosing. It just takes a decision, time, practice, and a little information about how to do it. My intention is to provide all the guidance you need in this book.

"Death is a passageway, not an ending. As I open my heart to continued connection, my beloveds are carried forward by my love."

Julia Cameron

Understanding How It Works

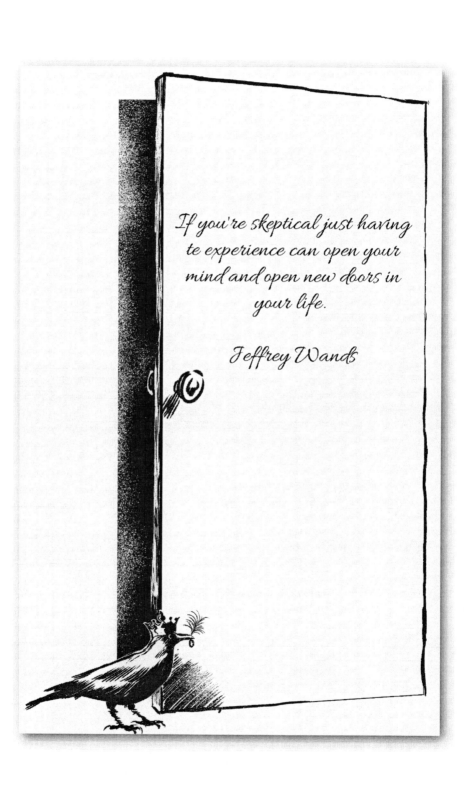

If you're skeptical just having te experience can open your mind and open new doors in your life.

Jeffrey Wands

The Door

When Nene announced to me, "I'm just on the other side of the door," three days after she died, I was startled to say the least. Now that my communication with her has been consistent for 11 years, I have come to discover so much more about what seemed like such a simple word "door."

A word that is often used in spiritual or "after death communication" (ADC) is portal. A portal is defined as a door, gate, or entrance, especially one of imposing appearance as a palace' and entry points. Obviously, a door leads from one room to another and, for our purposes, from one dimension to another or one world to another.

The implication in "I'm just on the other side of the door," as I understand it, is that there are two spaces that are intersected by a door or portal. As we live in this momentous time of spiritual evolution or intersection between heaven and earth, many of us can recall he phrase from The Lord's Prayer, "On earth as it is in heaven." I am discovering as I am writing, that opening these portals or doors between heaven and earth can open the floodgates through which the energies of heaven can come coursing onto earth. My vision is that as many of us facilitate the welcoming of the energies of heaven onto the earth through our loving connection with our loved ones, these connections can expand and open the floodgate portals between heaven and earth, therefore, fulfilling the promise "on earth as it is in heaven."

"The spirit world vibrates at an entirely different level from the physical world – it can't be registered by the eye, but it is rather felt and experienced by the mind when you start to exercise your awareness and pay close attention."

Sonia Choquette

11:11

I remember the first time I received validation about the number 11:11. I was on a trip into Telluride, Colorado. I purchased a book that called to me in a small bookstore on the way up the mountains. I was startled to find an entire chapter titled 11:11. I had been noticing 11:11 on clocks for a few years. I always felt some kind of a vibrational shift when I saw it. By this, I mean I felt more present, more alert, and highly tuned into the moment. This was several years before Nene transitioned. The book described an 11:11 sighting as a portal into another dimension. At this time, I certainly was not very clear about what "another dimension" meant. However, here it was, in black and white, a validation that what I had been experiencing was significant.

This became an opening for me. I began to pay closer attention when I saw these numbers. Whenever I saw 11:11, I paid close attention to what I was feeling in that moment.

Time passed and 11:11 sightings began turning into 11:11 conversations. I discovered that many people had an emotional reaction of some kind when they saw these numbers.

As this awareness and focus grew, I discovered meditation cards called 11:11, and a book written by the creators of the cards titled 11:11. This book gave examples of beliefs about this combination of numbers. The synopsis was that it has individual meaning to all who feel connected with it. Clearly, 11:11 was very significant to many people other than just me.

My connection with 11:11 was strong when Nene transitioned many years later. As my sister Cathy and I realized she had left her body, Cathy looked at the clock and stated 11:11. Her intention in doing this was to mark the time of her death. She was not aware of my relationship with these numbers and I did not mention it to her. I was the one in the family who was considered a little weird and this was not something that made sense to mention to anyone else at the time.

I continued, however, my research into the significance of these numbers and felt inspired to begin a search for books with 11:11 in the title. This was before I used the Internet and my personal search uncovered five books with the 11:11 in the title. I purchased all of them and began a study of this phenomenon. I am still learning about this, but it seems the most common interpretation of 11:11 is that it is a portal between dimensions.

"Once you begin connecting consciously to the unseen word, you can learn to speak its language. It's full of symbols, scents, riddles, jokes and even sounds – all of which are selected to mean something to you."

Sonia Choquette

As you create a connection with Spirit, the more you focus on it, the stronger it becomes.

Nenie Beanie

Why Do We Connect?

Those of us who are on a spiritual or metaphysical path have probably heard the statement, "The veils are thinning," As we continue our path of conscious evolution, we learn more about what this means. In ordinary language, it means that the division or separation between heaven and earth is going away.

We are here to create heaven on earth. Eckhart Tolle wrote about this in *The New Earth*, which was read by millions of people. The Lord's Prayer carries the words, "on earth as it is in heaven." We all know something is happening. We feel more love; we experience more synchronicity. Things are changing and they are changing fast.

We see so many books and movies about after death communication (ADC). This is becoming mainstream. We talk to each other more easily and more frequently about these things. Maybe this is not happening by accident. Maybe there is a purpose for this increased connection with other realms and our interest in knowing more about it.

As I turn my attention more consciously to Nene again, these thoughts surface.

Nene loves to make lists and it makes things so clear and concrete, so here is a playful listing of the whys and wherefores: the purpose of increased connection.

1) It inspires us to believe that there is more to life than what we can see and prove.
2) It supports our innate knowing that souls and spirits are real and continue after death.
3) It grows the Love. It allows us to consider and have the experience that the love we experienced for our loved ones does continue beyond death.
4) It is possible that those who have crossed over have gifts and resources that can assist us in creating heaven on earth.
5) We must focus inward to access our loved ones who have crossed over and as we do that, we become more adept at strengthening our relationship with our own spirits and souls
6) If Nene's last words "The circle of love is never broken" were true, then we are maintaining that Love through continuing to consciously connect with that love.
7) If Love is the most powerful force in the Universe, we are feeding and plugging into this force.

"Nothing scrambles psychic circuits and disconnects you from high frequencies faster and more completely than being judgmental or holding a grudge."

Sonia Choquette

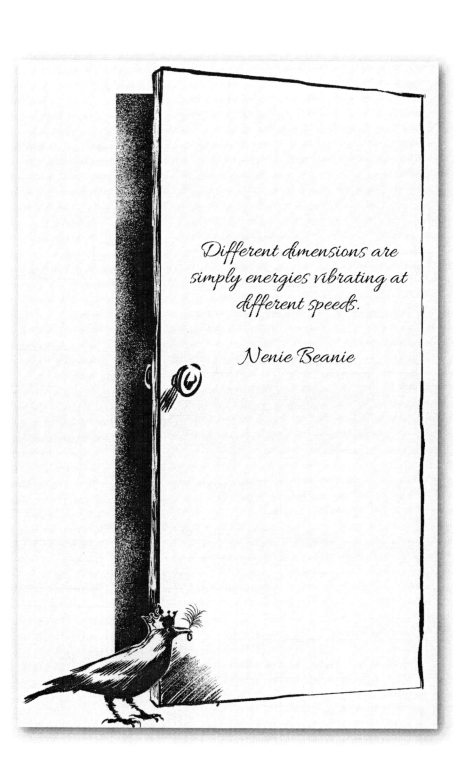

Different dimensions are simply energies vibrating at different speeds.

Nenie Beanie

PLANES OF EXISTENCE

Whenever I fly, I have a profound feeling of connection to Spirit as the plane rises into the sky and over the clouds. In a tangible way, this plane is taking me into an elevated state of being by rising high into the sky. We have heard the term "earthly plane", and we might have heard "heavenly plane" as well.

Language is so interesting to me because I am noticing this connection now that a plane (airplane) demonstrates the art of moving from one plane of existence to another.

Other phrases often used are "higher vibration or higher state of mind or elevated consciousness." All of us have had the experience of a higher state of consciousness. For some people this can be in church, with music or dance, loving a baby or a pet, or walks in the woods or by an ocean. Many experience this while meditating or watching a sunset or a full moon. This experience is a glimpse that all of us have had that is a higher plane of existence; some may call it a glimpse of heaven.

When we think of the "earthly plane", we often think of more mundane or material things. When we think of the heavenly plane, we imagine non-material like love, angelic music.

When someone dies or transitions, or crosses over, she simply moves from the earthly plane to the heavenly plane. Once there and immersed in these new higher energies, your loved one can direct these loving energies through your openness while residing in the material or earthly plane. This is not anything I can prove, but is an experience I have had with Nene.

One of my favorite spiritual teachings is that we are here to bring spirit into matter. This bridge that we can build with our loved one who has crossed over can become a channel through which this living, loving spirit can be brought onto the earthly plane.

This is, I believe, is a powerful avenue for creating heaven on earth. I believe the floodgates are opening and the opportunity to do this exists as has never before been available to us.

"If we recognize ourselves as spirit, we can more easily recognize the inhabitants of the non-physical world as well."

Sonia Choquette

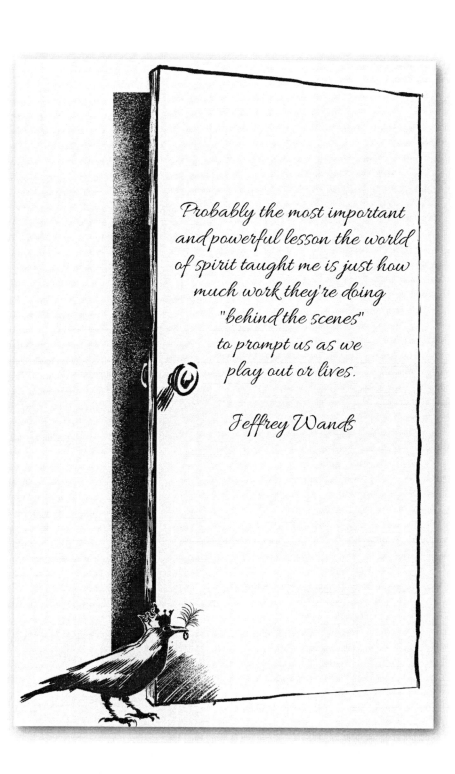

Probably the most important
and powerful lesson the world
of spirit taught me is just how
much work they're doing
"behind the scenes"
to prompt us as we
play out or lives.

Jeffrey Wands

"The Circle is Never Broken"

*T*hese were the last works spoken by Nene before she lapsed into a coma and died 24 hours later. What if this were true? What if she was speaking from a part of herself who was embarking on a journey into another plane of existence?

If Nene's words are true then our belief that death severs the loving connection would be inaccurate. If the loving connection continues after our loved one has left her body, then why not engage in behaviors to honor and grow these loving connections. What could it hurt? What harm could it do? People will think we are crazy? I suspect the more we talk about it the less crazy it will seem.

A study done by University of Chicago found that 42% of Americans have had an experience of connecting with a loved one after death and 94% Believe that life continues after death.

So, why not grow these loving connections? Growing love and expanding the "Circle of Love." How can this be wrong? Imagine the benefits of doing this. A well-accepted concept in metaphysical teachings and quantum physics is that, "What we focus on expands."

For the fun of it, here is a list of the benefits of believing and acting on this.

1) We would be moving our attention and focus toward the love in our hearts and by extending this to our loved one, we are creating a bridge between heaven and earth.

2) We would be calling up loving memories of our loved one, again expanding the expression and extension of love in our world; therefore spiritualizing the material world!

3) We would be moving our attention inward to our spirit and soul within, detaching ourselves temporarily from the material world. Our focus would be on our Inner World. Jesus said, "The kingdom of heaven is within you." We would be living there.

4) As we engage in these behaviors, we would be building energetic bridges between heaven and earth.

"All of life is interconnected and ongoing. There is no death to the spirit of those I love. As I mourn the physical passing of my beloveds, I open to meet them anew in an ongoing spiritual connection."

Julia Cameron

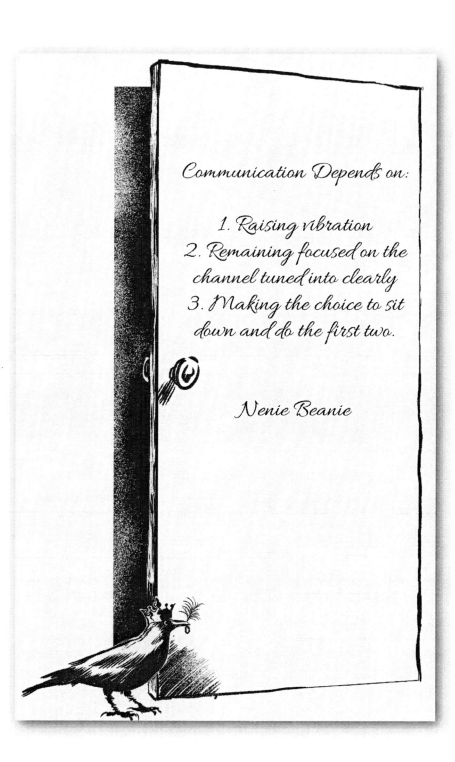

Communication Depends on:

1. Raising vibration
2. Remaining focused on the channel tuned into clearly
3. Making the choice to sit down and do the first two.

Nenie Beanie

Discovering IADC

As I was in the midst of writing the book, I found an opportunity to be trained in IADC, which stands for Induced After Death Communication. I had learned about it several years earlier, but synchronistically one of the handfuls of trainers lived in my city. I scheduled training with him and began reading Allan Botkin's book, *Induced After Death Communication,* in preparation for the training. Botkin is the developer of the IADC technique. He discovered it while using EMDR (a trauma reduction technique with veterans with PTSD (post-traumatic stress disorder).

My trainer, Cesar Valdez, greeted me in his serene loft office that overlooked downtown Ann Arbor on a beautiful midsummer day. Unknown to Cesar and I, dozens of vintage cars were lining up right below the window. Engines revving and loud mufflers blasting were part of the backdrop of what was to be my first IADC experience. Cezar apologized for the cacophony directly below us and asked if I thought I would be able to concentrate for the training and also have my first IADC session at the conclusion of our day. I told Cesar of a story Wayne Dyer had shared of attempting to meditate while being distracted by a landscaper with a Weed Whacker edging the lawn upon which his meditation mat was positioned. Dyer suddenly received the prompting, "use the sound of the Weed Whacker "as a mantra. So thanks to

Wayne Dyer I chose to use revving engines and mufflers as an aid in developing my meditative state as I had my first IADC session.

Hopefully, if you decide to try IADC with a certified facilitator, you will have a more peaceful setting.

"If you enter meditation with a completely open mind, it could be one of the greatest gifts you could give yourself. The key to remember is: The more you practices meditating, the better you will become, the more benefits you'll receive from it."

Patrick Matthews

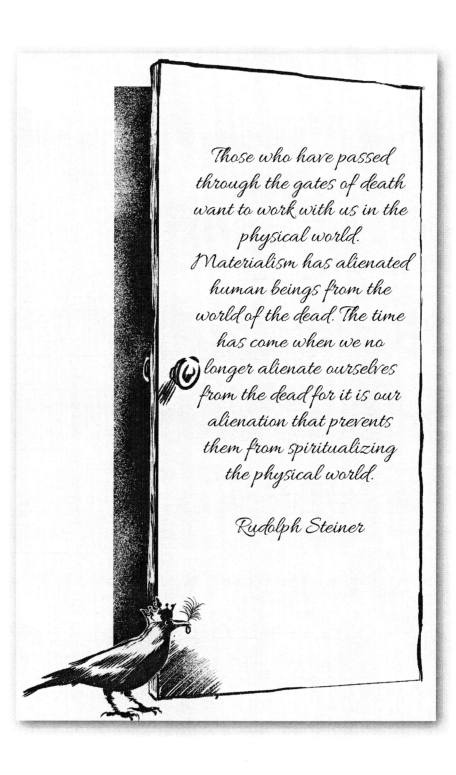

Those who have passed through the gates of death want to work with us in the physical world. Materialism has alienated human beings from the world of the dead. The time has come when we no longer alienate ourselves from the dead for it is our alienation that prevents them from spiritualizing the physical world.

Rudolph Steiner

SOUL TO SOUL

*M*ost people, regardless of their religion, spiritual beliefs, or lack thereof, believe that we have a soul. If you are reading this book and you do not believe you have a soul, I am probably not the one to convince you; so if you are of the opinion that the soul does not exist, continuing on might be a waste of your time.

In my experience of communicating with my sister, Nene, after her death, I believe I have come to be so much more connected to my soul. In fact, as I am now facilitating IADC procedures, I am coming to believe that the after death communication is a soul-to-soul connection. The Course in Miracles states, "We teach to learn." The more I write the more I recognize that I write to learn. I am exploring ways to assist the reader in experiencing their own ADC. Maintaining that connection and bringing more loving action into the world is my motive for writing this book.

As I continue to write and research, more and more concrete strategies and information about how to create connection with loved ones who have transitioned come into my awareness from countless sources.

The more I write the deeper this understanding becomes. It seems so clear that ADC is a soul-to-soul connection. How could it be otherwise? Here is how I think it works:

1) The loved one who has transitioned does not inhabit her/his body. The soul is consciousness that no longer is contained within a human

or animal body. To make a connection, it is necessary to have the ability to access your soul in order to be on the same wavelength or frequency or level of your loved one. You are obviously not fully in that dimension, as few have gone there completely and returned. The soul exists within a material world. To have a successful ADC, the temporary release of these material concerns and the connecting with the deep sense of peace, presence within is a prerequisite.

2) Tuning into the heart, the center of love, is a helpful way to access this energy. As one is immersed in the energy of love and focused on directing that love to the loved one on the other side of the door, a connection is made. The receptivity to open to whatever the loved one offers without expectation is another crucial piece of the ADC.

3) A third integral aspect of a successful ADC is remaining solidly in the present moment. In my writings with Nene, she focused on this necessary skill of holding strongly to the present moment.

I realized as I was reworking this section and staying receptive to Nene's energy, I had transitioned into making another list. Nene's passion for list making is woven throughout the book. As this naturally occurred, just now, as I was writing it offered another validation of Nene's very active participation in the writing.

As you connect with your loved one you are likely to find little signs or messages that confirm for you the reality of your connection. The more you do this the stronger the bridge of connection between you becomes and the more access you have to the love and messages from the other side of the door.

"Feeding your spirit on a regular basis helps you become aware of the spirit in all things, which opens the gateway to connecting ...."

Sonia Choquette

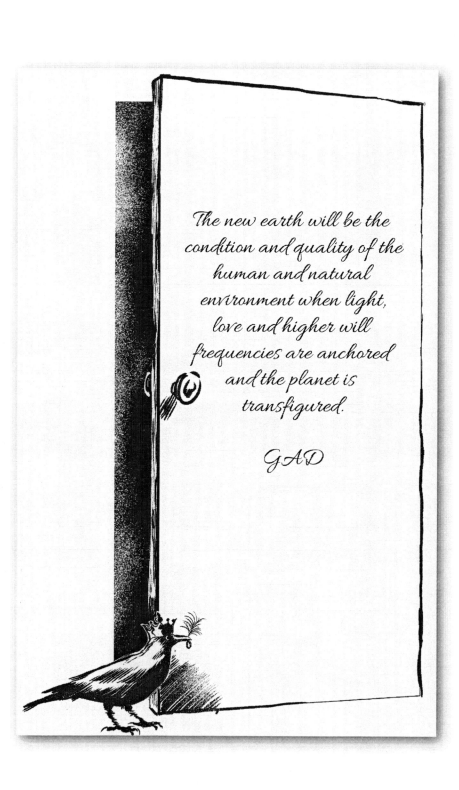

The new earth will be the condition and quality of the human and natural environment when light, love and higher will frequencies are anchored and the planet is transfigured.

GAD

What if We Knew? What if We Believed?

*T*his information is coming through directly and strongly from Nene right now. What if we knew, really knew that we are not alone? What if we knew we were surrounded by loved ones assisting us throughout each of our days? What if we believed that we were not left exclusively to our own limited knowledge, and skills, but had a huge unseen support team backing us – assisting us in all of our endeavors, thoughts and feelings? What if we knew that every room we sat in or walked into was filled with the spirits of our loved ones who had crossed over; our angels; our guides? What a different life experience we would have.

I just wrote what was coming through directly from Nene. It was being scribed by me, however, and maybe somewhat filtered. (I am human after all) I realize as I write this that if I believed it and lived this way I would have an entirely different life experience. Einstein said, "The most important question is, "Is the universe friendly?" What if the Universe were friendlier than we could ever possibly imagine? What if each of us was surrounded by indescribably loving intelligent beings? What if we believed and acted accordingly? What would happen to your sense of powerlessness? How would you behave differently? How would we take action? How would we feel when we woke up in the morning? How would we feel going to bed at night having lived our day with this awareness and acted accordingly? How would we feel about our ability to impact the world in a positive way? What a different world it would be. What if we each discovered our passion and acted on it with the heartfelt knowledge that we were not alone and there were powerful energies supporting posed and ready to assist and us. If we really believed this, really knew it, we could change the world. Simply suspending judgments and opening to such an extraordinary possibility could only have monumental results.

My intuition has been telling me that we are on the cusp of a "Great Uprising." The separation between the third and fourth dimension is dissolving. Our access to these loved ones who have crossed over has exponentially expanded. My belief is that these loved ones are not only poised and ready to assist us individually, but they are ready and equipped to help us all on a planetary scale.

What if each of us looked for what part we wanted to play in bringing heaven to earth and knew that we had unfathomable assistance from the other side as we played our part.

What if we each discovered our passion and acted on it with the heartfelt knowledge that there were loving energies powerfully supporting us. That we have loved ones who are constantly poised to assist us? We could change the world. We could create heaven on earth.

What if we each discovered our passion and acted on it with the heartfelt knowledge that those spirits were POWERFULLY supporting us, and loved ones who are constantly poised to assist us? We could change the world. We could create heaven on earth.

Writing this book has been virtually effortless. It's as if I've had a powerful back-wind moving me forward at warp speed. I strongly suspect this has been my own personal experience with working with these supportive energies. Why not give it a try? What do you have to lose?

Almost all indigenous cultures include some kind of relationship with "the ancestors." Our western culture has eliminated the belief that our relationships continue to exist after they have left physical form. Maybe now is the time to rediscover these connections and use these relationships in the service of creating a better world.

"We must learn to see the dead not as deceased but living among us human beings who share our life and work."

Rudolf Steiner

As these frequencies are
raised into a higher
dimensional vibration
through the absorption of
light and love, the spiritual
worlds become perceptible
as a realm of experience
for humanity.

Gordon Asher Davidson

FROM DOORWAY TO FLOODGATES

When I had my first experience of connecting with Nene in August 2004, her words were "I'm just on the other side of the door."

Now after 11 years of connecting and countless experiences, I am feeling more like "the floodgates between heaven and earth are being flung wide open." I believe the reason for this exponentially expanded opening is timing. Jean Houston states, "We are living at the most important time in human history. This is the time that *we* decide whether we live or whether we die." Numerous religious teachings see this as a time of enormous planetary evolution. The words conscious evolution and new earth are becoming mainstream. We all can see and feel that something huge is happening.

Years ago, I received a powerful message in meditation. It was "At this crucial time in human history, whoever can be used will be used to the highest level possible." Little did I realize that those who could be used, were willing to, would be the countless number of loved ones who had crossed over into the world of spirit.

To accommodate the "great uprising," we require floodgates rather than doors. What I believe is the accessibility to loved ones who have crossed over is unprecedented. We have an opportunity to be used to facilitate our loved ones being used in the service of creating heaven on earth in a way that never existed before. '

These energies will continue to expand exponentially as each of us plugs into and builds these energetic bridges. The Hopi Prophesy that closes with, "We are the ones we've been waiting for," can be expanded to include our loved ones who continue to exist and love from the non-material world.

What were once doorways are rapidly transforming into floodgate.

"Awakening to our own intuitive powers is more important than ever because I believe that humanity is going through a meta-morphosis – from a material world to a spiritual one."

Char Margolis

CROWS

*O*ne morning within the first year of Nene's death, I was writing to her sitting on a porch swing that she used to love. As I wrote, four crows sitting in a nearby tree began cawing so loudly and persistently it was impossible to ignore them.

I moved my attention to them and tuned in more closely to my communication with Nene. As I did, I heard the message, "I am as close to you as these crows are. We both fly back and forth between dimensions"

The clarity of that message was so strong that I began experiencing crows as a message from Nene that she was nearby. Whenever I heard or saw a crow, I intentionally tuned into Nene.

This became something that I trusted more and more as I consistently communicated with Nene. In doing this, the crow became a symbol for my connection with her. One day I purchased a beautiful crow statue and was prompted to put a tiara on it, as this was a reminder of a special memory of Nene that demonstrated her humor and light-heartedness.

Within the final few months before Nene transitioned, she requested a party of all her loved ones requiring formal attire. She wore on her head throughout the event a beautiful rhinestone tiara. In preparation for the party, I asked Nene if she would like a cake. She gave me a mischievous smile and teased, "What do you want to write on it; Happy Death Day? This is an example of Nene's playful acceptance of her upcoming death. In the last few weeks before she left she sat on the porch swing with me and mused, "I always knew I was going to die, but I didn't know it was going to take so long."

Nene used the 14 years of a terminal diagnosis as a catalyst for creating a profound spiritual connection. When she left this dimension, she was fully prepared for the trip.

Now that Nene and I are communicating between dimensions, I am intent on increasing my effectiveness in doing this. One of the things I have learned is that the more I do it the easier and stronger the connection becomes. One of the things Nene said in our communication was "There's a bridge!!! A bridge and a channel are similar. We are connecting from one dimension to another. The channel allows the information to flow through like electricity. All you have to do is turn on the switch. Open your end of the channel and let the information flow through to you."

As I reread and prepared to finish this piece, a cluster of crows began cawing loudly and swooping back and forth outside my patio door. This was unusual because it was 7:30 in the morning on a snowy 20-degree day. I felt such intense gratitude to Nene and tuned in even more intently.

What came is that this is a perfect time to describe the process of using a symbol to align your energy with a vibration you want to plug into. As I created in my mind the perception that the crow was a symbol of my connection with Nene, I created an opening for connecting with her. Each time I do this, I strengthen the bridge and broaden the channel that connects from her to me and me to her. This is a great description of how using a symbol and tuning in through that symbol strengthens your ability to connect with your loved one and invite the energies of heaven onto this earth plane.

As you are preparing to connect with your loved one, being open to noticing signs and symbols that grow your feelings of connection can be an important part of your process.

"Today, I am brave enough to open to continued connection. I am alert to small signs and signals which speak to me of my beloveds' ongoing presence."

Julia Cameron

CROWS II

When I was returning from my walk with my dog, Dexter this morning the most magnificent crow swooped down into my line of vision and perched herself halfway up the tree I was approaching. She sat there for a full minute as I gazed at her, feeling awestruck at her beauty. She then flew to another tree landing significantly higher and posed there for another minute or so. My sense of wonder continued to grow as she then launched herself higher and then swooped down below the roofline on the backside of my house.

As I drew in a deep breath of satisfaction and reverence, I knew that it was Nene reminding me to write and connect with her this morning. So, here I am writing and connecting to Nene, to myself, and to you dear reader, as you take in these words.

Writing can be an amazing process of putting your heart, soul, feelings and awareness's on the page for others to read. It is actually quite a courageous act and one that is not performed without a certain amount of fear and resistance. What will you think? Will you judge me? Will I inspire you? That is my intention.

So, here I am, expounding about a crow flying by. It does, however, have so much meaning for me. I am reminded of an idea I heard once that what is most important about almost anything is the meaning we give to it. Perception is everything. My intention is that my experience with my perception of my ongoing connection with Nene will be a catalyst for your looking more deeply into the experiences in your life.

In my book *Sacred Marching Orders,* I wrote a piece called, "Plugging into the Energy of Awe." I have learned through my paying attention that: catching oneself in moments of awe and consciously plugging into that energy field assists you in your desire to return "Home to the Oneness." What could be a better way to support our tuning into the Oneness than connecting with a precious loved one who resides there all the time?

Probably all of us have experienced or heard someone say that watching a sunset or a velvet carpet of stars at night elicits in us an awareness of the vastness and oneness of the Universe.

I have learned that a way that works for me is my tuning into the crows as messengers from my sister, Nene, who resides on the other side of the door. The meaning I assign to it is a powerful, beautiful, awe-inspiring connection. It works for me and we all have our own unique individual ways of finding meaning. I support you in your search for meaning.

"*Pay attention to all the subtle clues that enter your awareness, and don't wait for the spiritual equivalent of Elvis to appear, while dismissing all the rest. Spirit guidance is subtle, so it's up to you to raise your awareness enough to acknowledge and accept their help as it's offered.*"

Sonia Choquette

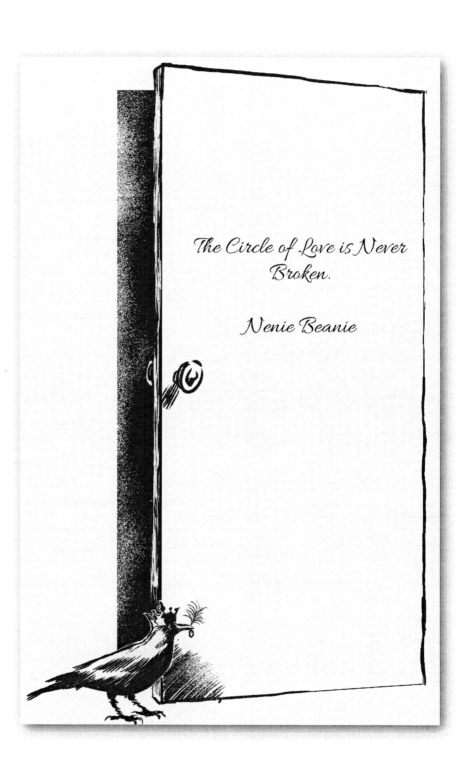

The Circle of Love is Never Broken.

Nenie Beanie

SYNCHRONICITY

As the book was almost completed, I attended a retreat led by Jean Shinoda Bolen, a wise woman writer and teacher who has been my primary mentor since I found her first book, *The Tao of Psychology Synchronicity and the Self* in the early 80's.

I knew it was going to be a powerful weekend, but it was impossible for me to even imagine how events would unfold.

Although I was finished writing, there was one small pesky piece that I still had not been able to get quite right. My inner guidance told me that the solution to how to write this section would be revealed during our sessions.

We began Friday night and the momentum began to build. Jean was magical and embodied the brilliance that changes the energy in any setting. I was poised on the edge of my seat absorbing every piece of information she shared with us about archetypes and Greek mythology.

When I returned to my hotel room that night, I began to get little bits and pieces of ideas about how I would redo this final writing. As I write "Ms. Right" showed up with her misspells so I received stronger confirmation. Nene was strongly guiding me, also.

Saturday morning began with great anticipation and the intensity of the energy in the room as palpable. When we recessed for lunch, I seized the opportunity to speak briefly with Jean. I thanked her for her endorsement of my second book *What Happens When Women Wake Up?* I told her the title and topic of this book and she pensively remarked, "I wonder if the other side" is something we should talk about after lunch." I could not quite believe my ears and did my best to encourage that amazing possibility. In speaking at the end of lunch she said, "I know you're ready but I'm not so sure about everybody else." I understood and returned to the reconvened session expecting more amazing knowledge about archetypes. She began with her topic and spoke for about 45 minutes. She then paused, closed her eyes, clearly turning her attention inward. She asked the group, "How many of you have had an experience with a loved one who crossed over." Forty-eight of the 50 women raised their hands! She then shared powerful experiences of her own connection with a loved one who had died. This was moving and very personal.

At her lead and request, one woman after another shared their stories of contacts with loved one who had crossed over, including beloved pets. The circle of women was now in a timeless state of loving connection.

She invited us all to invite our loved ones into the circle and the change in the energy in the room was breathtaking. I teased that Nene was having great fun, as she has always been very playful.

This was a peak experience for me. In reporting the event to my friends, I said, "It was like having my birthday, Christmas, and every other celebration rolled into one." I could not have received a more powerful and miraculous validation and encouragement that we are ready for this information.

In this magical afternoon, I believed I had so much tangible from "the other side of the door." That pesky little piece could not have been completed because it had not happened yet.

"But death isn't as serious as you think it is, honey. So far, it's very enjoy-able. Couldn't be better, really. Try not to take death too seriously."

Annie Kagan
The Afterlife of Billy Fingers

Accessing Spirit

Heaven is energy from the inside. The more you allow yourself to experience it, the deeper or higher you will go.

Nenie Beanie

Having a Place

*Y*esterday when I was writing out here at the cottage, I felt a stronger than usual connection with Nene. I asked her what she suggested writing about (remember we are writing this together). What came was "make a list." Nene was definitely "the list girl" and I accepted this prompt and began making a list as I felt was being dictated by her. What it turned out to be was a new table of contents that perfectly arranged all the writings I have completed up to this point.

Every piece fit into its own category perfectly with the exception of three sections titled "The Cottage, the Pond, and the Deck." This morning while having a soul-to-soul talk with my friend, Lauri, it became clear that these writings belonged in their own chapter titled, "Having a Place." My cottage is an environment where I am able to connect with spirit often, specifically Nene, most powerfully. Eckhart Tolle states *In the New Earth*, "Only spirit can communicate with spirit." In order to have the experience of connecting with a loved one who has crossed over, one must be able to access one's own spirit. The loved one is no longer in the form of a body but now exists in spirit. Spirit to spirit communication requires accessing that spirit within.

Having a place is an extremely effective way to support the accessing of your own spirit. In my phone call with Lauri this morning, we explored how we move ourselves into energy or a state of consciousness or presence. These are difficult states to describe, but they are crucial to understanding so I am going to do my best to convey what each of these is.

We're (Nene and I) going to do our best here by attempting to make the abstract concrete and describe concepts that are helpful in connecting with one's spirit in the form of a list. We'll start with energy.

1) Energy. I have not looked up the dictionary definition of energy, but most of us are familiar with the slang word vibe. Whenever we are around anyone, if we pay attention we can identify the "vibe" we are picking up. We may feel drawn or repelled. We may feel peaceful or anxious. We may feel happy or kind of depressed. The vibe that we are feeling from that person is a result of the energy that person is emitting. As I write this, I am acutely aware this is just a glimpse of what I mean when I use the word energy, but maybe it is enough for you to clarify your own sense of how you understand energy in this context. So the energy we want to create in our special place are energies of being still; being in the moment and undisturbed by the outside world.

2) State of Consciousness. I see consciousness as awareness, but in this context, it is awareness of one's inner world. This includes not being focused on the material world. The thoughts that parade through our heads, the attachment to material things are temporarily suspended. The inner awareness is an experience of releasing the outer world. This is a sense that is similar to the feeling of floating in a raft in smooth, open waters with a warm sun shining down. Achieving this state takes practice; meditation seems to be the most effective technique for accessing this state of consciousness.

3) The Presence. For me the Presence is a state of consciousness in which one's attachment to the material world or the outside, the world of form is temporarily suspended. My experience is that Presence is being totally and completely still. To me, it is almost palpable. It feels like time and space is suspended and the connection with the present moment is secure and uninterrupted by thought or distraction of any kind. Several years ago in my writing to Nene, she advised me, "Plant

yourself in the present." This gave me a helpful visual as I saw a flower with a root going deep into the earth, the face turned upward to absorb the rays of the sun. Trees are our greatest teachers of experiencing the present by standing tall, rooted deeply in the earth with branches reaching silently but powerfully into the sky.

Having a place means having a chair, a room, a cottage, a place in the woods or anywhere where you can consistently tap into your energy, move into a state of consciousness; and practice the presence or present—doing this consistently will strengthen your capacity for connecting with and maintaining a connection with your loved one who now lives in spirit rather than a body.

Spirit to spirit is the only way. Accessing your spirit is the work that is yours to do. The potential exists and the rewards are immeasurable.

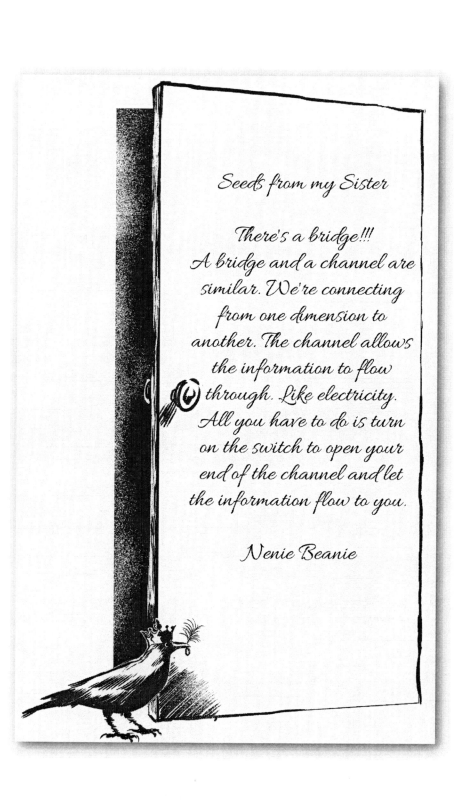

Seeds from my Sister

There's a bridge!!!
A bridge and a channel are
similar. We're connecting
from one dimension to
another. The channel allows
the information to flow
through. Like electricity.
All you have to do is turn
on the switch to open your
end of the channel and let
the information flow to you.

Nenie Beanie

The Cottage

As I connected with Nene early in June out at my cottage, she shared these words with me, "The cottage is the answer. Spend lots of time here this summer." Writing this in early August, I was reminded of the summer at the cottage that I spent going through the boxes of writings with her that ultimately became the "Seeds from My Sister" meditation cards. Leah, my collaborator, and I spent countless hours on the living room floor of the cottage matching quotes from Nene with Leah's macro shots of nature. Leah and I both knew that the cottage carried a powerful energy and we immersed ourselves in that energy most weekends of that summer. This place was where I most deeply connected with my soul, wrote to Nene most effectively and completed my book, *What Happens When Women Wake Up?* Earlier this year I discovered Glenn Aparicio Parry's book *Original Thinking*. In it, he describes differences between Western perspectives and indigenous ways of being. I was particularly intrigued by the idea that Western culture tends to focus on linear time, past and future, while indigenous connects more to place.

This concept prompted me to attend more to my relationship with the cottage and the magnificent piece of land on which it sits. The time that I have spent here each summer for the last 10 years have created an experience of presence or access to my soul that I don't experience as frequently during my busy work week or activity filled weekends spent in Ann Arbor.

My experience of love, expansiveness leisure, pleasure and quiet reflection create the connection for a deep well of creative inspiration.

Being in the moment listening to the breeze flutter the poplar leaves in the center of the yard, hearing the cicadas, and the crows cawing perform a natural symphony of sounds we have little access to in the city.

What a backdrop for my tuning into my inner ear and letting the words flow through my pen. Connecting with loved ones who have crossed over is a soul-to-soul connection. Any avenues to contact with one's soul is a way to increase the possibility of an after death connection or a successful IADC. As you read my love letter to the cottage what comes to your mind as a place or an experience that facilitates your connection with your soul?

"Anything that is done creatively, be it writing, music, drawing, cooking, planting, etc., can also include connecting with loved ones on the other side.
... Being in this state is an excellent time for connecting to the other side."

Patrick Matthews

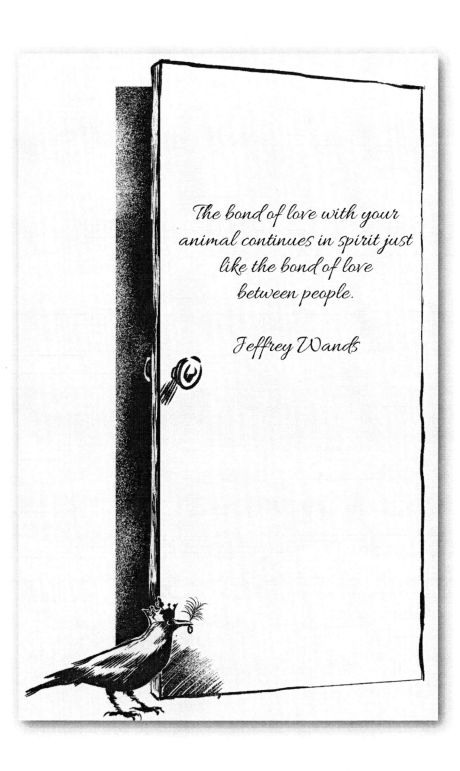

The bond of love with your
animal continues in spirit just
like the bond of love
between people.

Jeffrey Wands

THE POND

This morning on the deck of the cottage, I just kept looking at this shaded area of grass on the edge of the pond. I was having an amazing conversation with my friend, Lauri, about these spiritual energies we both love to tune into and create inspiring conversations and new awareness's. My connection with other dimensions was deepening as we let ourselves meander from one topic to another, but allowing insights, intuitions, and guidance continue to be the energy that we stayed with. I told her that when I ended the call I was going to move my porch swing out to the shaded spot by the water and read Sonia Coquette's book, *Ask your Guides.* Sonia has an amazing history of being aware of communicating with her guides from the beginning of her life. Sonia's mother had done the same and supported her daughter's experiences. A comment in her book brought home powerfully an idea that I am beginning to understand as I am writing this book. She wrote, "As an adult, I've come to believe that our disconnection from the spirit world is a western soul disease. Industrialization and intellectualism have snatched our center of awareness from our hearts—the place where we meet and commune with our spirit— and planted it squarely in our heads, where our eyes reign over us with threats of isolation and annihilation. The good news is that whatever reason for the separation, we can reconnect our inner awareness back to our hearts—if we want to, and if we don't allow our minds to hold us completely hostage."

As I read this concept, a fascinating insight popped into my awareness. IADC has been supported by thousands of documented experiences, but no one fully understands why it works. What occurred to me out by the pond is that when we are in a highly tuned in receptive state of being, and when someone is feeling their sadness by using EMDR to move through their grief, they are powerfully connected to their heart. The heart is clearly where we carry our sadness. A broken heart is a universal phrase for extreme sadness. As the client processes through his or her sadness and continues with the EMDR in a quiet receptive state of being, the bridge, door or portal of the spirit world is present from heart to heart.

My first IADC experience was with my dog, Daisy, who crossed over on 11/5/13. The most significant aspect of the connection was that I experienced a tube of light about four inches in diameter that formed a bridge connected our two hearts. This transfusion and exchange of light love continued for about three to five minutes. The experience was unquestionable and, as I described it to my teacher, Cesar, saying I had no doubt about the reality of it he showed a quote by a Jungian analyst, Frances Vaughan. She stated, "Truth is not learned; it is recognized."

Now as I am following the flow of the words marinating in the beautiful energy in my porch swing by the pond, I am wondering if this experience with Daisy was a clue to me of how I can help increase the success of clients who are seeking an IADC experience.

Life is amazing when you consciously tune in; remain receptive to what wants to show up. It is a great way to live.

"Animals move between dimensions so much more readily than you humans do. Most indigenous people know that."

Nenie Beanie

This infusion of higher
energies allows all life to
function within more subtle
spiritual levels, while also
retaining the capacity to
function in the physical,
emotional and
mental worlds.

Gordon Asher Davidson

SITTING ON THE DECK

I asked Nene to talk with me. I plugged in and listened and now I am writing. It is that easy. Connecting; tuning in; listening; and letting the words flow through your pen. As I write, I am remembering an upcoming workshop titled "Inspired Writing". I did not invent this practice. I discovered it, and like any significant discovery, it has had monumental impact on my many people. I was recently reading a book titled, *Evolutionaries* by Carter Phillips, and read a section about how human history is not just a collection of dates and events and periods, but a developmental process in which one stage creates a foundation and becomes integrated into the next stage and continues to grow and change as humanity moves forward. This is a global description of what psychologists have understood about individual human development. Each person moves through each stage beginning in infancy and, as she or he masters or doesn't, the next forms the foundation for the proceeding one. Developmental Psychology teaches, for example, the building on one stage after the others includes an integration of the former lessons and beliefs of the previous stage.

As I am writing this, guided by Nene, reflecting on the integration between the two of us in our 11 years of communication, I wonder what does this have to do with what I want to convey in this book. I still don't know, but I am staying tuned in, paying attention, listening to my greatest ability, remembering to stay in the moment and let the words flow without looking for or listening ahead. As I do this, I notice that it is a practice that I have developed over thousands of hours of connecting to Nene.

Now I am beginning to get little clues about the relevance. I began in 2004, not knowing much of anything about what I was doing, I heard about the idea of writing to a loved one who had crossed over or talking to your angels several years prior. Continuing to do this day after day and year after year, I have had countless experiences that validate the value of the process and the truth of the connection. Most significantly now for me, it is a felt sense of presence that is very different from my everyday functioning in my daily life. I know it, I feel it, but I cannot prove it.

The inspiration for, me in, in writing this book is that as we develop the practice of tuning in deeply and regularly with loved ones who have died, we can access valuable resources to assist all of humanity in our evolution from quite limited human beings to more expansive and loving spiritual beings who combine the best of humanity and spirituality. I believe that this inter-dimensional communication is one of our wonderful next steps in our human-spiritual evolution.

"Communication does not stop at the doorway of death. The wall between physical reality and spirit is really very thin."

Pat Rodegast & Judith Stanton
<u>Emmanuel's Book</u>

Concepts To Consider

*All the teachings speak
about being still,
slowing down,
going deep.*

Nenie Beanie

THE MOMENT

As I was writing to Nene this morning, I asked her what she wanted to say. She suggested we write another piece for the book. I asked her what she wanted to write about. She said, "Just start writing." So I did. The title came immediately "The Moment." I continually became aware of the thought of "trusting the moment." Now I realize experientially what I have heard so many times: the spiritual teaching that each moment is different. We have these ideas about the past and the future. I am clear that they are concepts that help us navigate the earth plane. Now I am recognizing the truth that life, eternity exists in this one moment and each moment. A beautiful example is that of the magic of a snowflake. Each one is different, unique in its own way, never to come again.

What is coming to me now is that connecting with a loved one who resides in eternity, outside of time, is a reinforcement of our capacity to live in that state ourselves. As we connect with the energy or vibration of our loved one existing in eternity, we are stepping into the ocean of eternity ourselves and swimming around there for a while.

Although Eckhart Tolle says that he lives in the moment all the time, most of us have not reached that level of awakening yet. (See how I slip back into time comparisons so quickly?) My humanity is still present. I do believe, however, that the more I infuse my humanity with my spirit self, the more my spirit comes to be expressed in each moment.

Deepak Chopra gave a beautiful example in one of his many books about how we come into our spiritual selves. He described taking a red handkerchief and rinsing it in the river and hanging it to dry in the sun. He explained that every time we do this day after day the red cloth becomes lighter until ultimately it become totally white. I think he was describing the effects of regular meditation. Clearly, this is true, but I also believe that connecting with loved ones in the energy of eternity creates the same effect on our souls.

So Nene's suggestion to me, "Just begin writing," got me to a new, stronger awareness of the value of connecting with her in the present moment, trusting her wisdom in her eternal reality, letting the words flow and unfold from this energy. What a gift.

"Here, each moment flows into the next so you wind up with that 'eternity' feeling."

Annie Kagan
The Afterlife of Billy Fingers

Plant yourself in the present.

Nenie Beanie

Practicing the Presence

This is the title of a book written by mystic, Joel Goldsmith. I always loved the title. I was attracted to it. The words drew me in, but when I first encountered the book, I had only a vague sense of what those words meant. Now, 11 years after first connecting with Nene, I know this feeling in a way that is profound and palpable.

I learned through my countless hours of writing with Nene that I could only access her if I was fully connected to the present moment. A phrase that she gave me that stays with me and supports my connection with her, which was: "Plant yourself in the present."

I love this phrase because it is so easy to create a visual of a plant or tree with roots that grow deep into the earth. When I remind myself of this simple phrase, the more often I do it the more deeply I am able to draw in the energy of the present moment.

When I just first began writing, I experienced yet another misspell that is a strong message that I am getting input from Nene. She was reminding me of another phrase she gave me when I was struggling with keeping my energy and attention in the moment, she said to me "Dash ahead - dash ahead - dash your head." Receiving these words from Nene made me laugh out loud as I was sitting there writing to her. I understood that this comical directive to "Dash my head" was referring to my propensity to so frequently rush into the next moment. She was educating me of the necessity of letting go of my thoughts, judgments and predictions so that I could remain in the moment and be an open vessel for her words to flow into. As you learn more about how to connect with loved ones on the other side you will continue to understand that the suspension of judgment and thoughts is crucial in making the connection.

The words "dash ahead and dash your head" are so pointed in their direction to stay in the present, let go of the thinking process, including suspending judgment, moving your attention out of your head.

Because I love to make this concrete and Nene loves to make lists, here is a crib note on how to move into an experience of a sense of presence:

1) Plant yourself in the present.
2) Suspend judgment.
3) Let go of thinking.
4) Practice, practice, practice.

Just like any physical exercise or developing any skill, the more you practice, the more you develop a full sense of the experience. Practicing the presence or the present creates the required inner hardware to create the connection with loved ones who reside in the unseen realms.

Just as you cannot tune into a television station without having a working television, so you cannot access the energies from where they are transmitting without making yourself a functional receiver.

Practicing the presence and planting yourself in the present, is the most effective way to do this. As you develop those abilities, you will become more and more adept. You will recognize that state of presence and become proficient at maintaining it and deepening it.

"Dying is akin to having been in a rather stuffy room where too many people are talking and smoking and suddenly you see a door that allows you to exit into fresh air and sunlight. Truly it is much like that."

Pat Rodegast & Judith Stanton
Emmanuel's Book

Souls come from the sea of love to wander about continually seeking return to that sea of love with vaguest memory of where they came from.

Nenie Beanie

PERCEPTION

*M*any years ago, long before I began on a conscious spiritual path, I saw a poster of a big shaggy dog whose eyes were completely covered by his long fur. The caption read, "I always see better with my heart." Thirty years later, I still have a strong memory of that image.

I have learned and continue to understand more deeply that, "seeing through the heart" is the most reliable way to create a connection with a loved one who has crossed over.

My state of being when I connect consciously with Nene is an every-expanding experience of profound love. This has been a discovery that has been gradual over the last 11 years. I loved her so much and this was a starting point, but my written communications with her after she left her body have taught me that the more I focus on my love for her and feel her love for me the stronger and clearer the connection becomes.

How we perceive and what we perceive is determined by where we put our attention on. The *Course in Miracles* teaches that there are only two emotions, love or fear, and we choose what we experience by where we put our attention or focus.

I believe connection with a loved one who crosses over is a soul-to-soul contact. It follows logically that if we place our attention on the profound love that is the essence of our soul we can access the soul of our loved ones who no longer reside in a physical body.

Listening opens the door to everything that matters.

Mark Nepo

Listening Intently to the Inside

Developing the capacity to connect with loved ones who have crossed over is a practice. Practice is a word we hear often in spiritual circles and conversation. "What is your practice?" is a question that is routine in this world. I am coming to understand as I explore how to communicate this skill of connecting with loved ones on the other side that is a profound spiritual practice.

We live in a world that focuses almost exclusively on the outer or material aspects of life. The understanding of, or even awareness of an inner world is actually quite rare. Last week in a psychotherapy session, I drew out a diagram of a person illustrating the inner and outer worlds of all of us.

Surprisingly, as the client and I constructed the diagram together I noticed that there was so much more content in the inner world than the outer. The inner world includes our thoughts, feelings, beliefs, and emotions like love. I am learning that the feelings of love from the heart creates the bridge. Practicing connecting from the heart is the most important thing you can do.

Contacting one who is no longer in material form requires an entry point from ones' own inner world. The traditional communication through the outer world is no longer an option, but it is still possible to communicate with someone once one has left the material world.

Then we have to develop a practice of connecting with our inner world. It seems to me that using one's own creativity and intuition, as a starting point, would be the most effective. As you reflect on your inner feelings or emotions, what words from the inside world are you most drawn to? Maybe you could use these as an entry point by choosing one or two and focusing on or paying attention to these.

This is where practice comes in. In spiritual circles "practice" is often seen as a noun, such as "What is your Practice?" For our purposes, in beginning, I suggest seeing practice as a verb, as in "practicing the piano." We are beginners now, most of us, so we practice every day to improve our skills in connecting with our inner world. As we become more adept, we can move into the experience of connecting with our loved ones *as* a spiritual practice. We have to learn the scales and the notes before we can play a concerto.

My intention in writing this book is to provide the skills needed to learn how to connect with loved ones who have crossed over. Additionally I believe they have so much to offer our world and us. As we create the practice of connecting and communicating, we can bring through such love and resources that are not accessible to us without conscious contact.

The only pathway is through the inner world and this takes intention, focus, and practice. I believe the rewards are immeasurable.

"Our intuitive sense is literally a channel between this world and the next. It is an energy conduit through which we can connect with loved ones who have died."

Char Margolis

Nothing is more important than raising your vibration.

Nenie Beanie

READINESS

As I have been facilitating IADCs, I am beginning to learn more about readiness and waiting. We live in such an action-oriented culture. Performance and success is revered. Patience and silence are not considered to be aspects of "getting ahead" and accomplishments.

In my IADC training, my facilitator, Cesar, said he wished it was not called induced after death communication. Both he and Allan Botkin, the psychotherapist who wrote the book called *Induced After Death Communication*, and who originally discovered this technique have learned through experience that attempting to push or anticipate, or try to create an IADC was more likely to prevent one than cause it. I am also observing that as I am practicing this teaching with my clients.

I had a startling experience with a friend years ago. She was gardening for the first time and she was so anxious to find out if her seeds were taking root that she dug one up. I was aghast as I watched this. Her inability to relax and trust the process was shocking to observe. You can imagine the effect on the seedling that had been uprooted.

This is an example of qualities required to have a successful IADC; relaxing and trusting the process. Your task is to create the fertile soil from which the experience can emerge to create a state of receptivity.

This way of being is so counter to our Western, especially American way of functioning. Our fore fathers tilled the land, mined the earth, cleared the forests, built the houses, and wiped out an entire people, the original inhabitants of North America. All of this was done in the name of progress and accomplishment. Settling into the silence and allowing are foreign concepts to this Western value of working hard and taking action. My intention in the writing is not to malign the Western way but to clarify the difference in the two different ways of experiencing.

One is doing and the other is being. Cultivating the state of being is not only the way to increase the likelihood of having an IADC, but it is also the primary way to increase your experience of presence in your daily life, and to increase your ability to connect with spirit on a regular basis.

When I began writing this book, I was unaware of Botkin's work with IADC. My intention was to assist readers in learning how to connect with loved ones who had transitioned through writing. Now, having been trained, and practicing the facilitation of IADC myself I am so enthusiastic about this technique for making contact.

My wish is to support those who choose to access a therapist who facilitates IADC to be successful with their process.

"Unpredictable as life itself, the practice of listening is one of the most mysterious, luminous, and challenging art forms on earth."

Mark Nepo

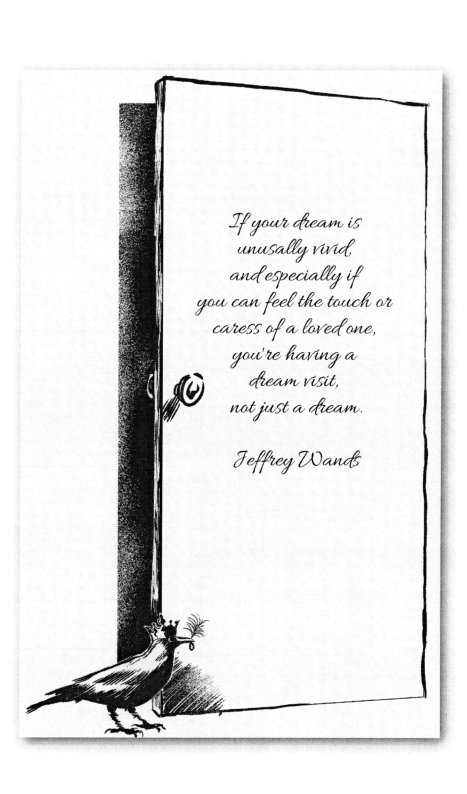

If your dream is
unusally vivid,
and especially if
you can feel the touch or
caress of a loved one,
you're having a
dream visit,
not just a dream.

Jeffrey Wands

SELF-TRUST

I came across a TED talk this morning that was about change. I think quoting Gandhi's famous words "Be the Change." A young 20-something man spoke about living his early life following the rules and doing what was expected of him gave the talk. This included beginning in college, feeling depressed and directionless. He began seeing a therapist who encouraged him to feel his feelings and connect with what he wanted to do. He decided to leave college, much to his parent's dismay, and began a journey of self-discovery. He did what Joseph Campbell suggested, "Follow your bliss." In doing this he is now doing life changing social activism, he is living his passion. There are countless examples of people choosing this path of doing what they want to do rather than what they were told to do.

We are socialized to trust others and rely on what comes from the outside rather than what comes from our own inner world. Many people are not even aware of what this is. Trusting oneself from the inside out is a crucial aspect to having a connection with a loved one who has crossed over.

As you practice embodying some of the qualities described in this part of the book, you will develop an increased ability to trust yourself. You will develop increased ability to trust yourself. Believing in what comes from the inside more than what comes from the outside is an aspect of self-trust.

Heaven is being in a loving state here and now.

Nenie Beanie

RECEPTIVITY

As I was spending a little morning time at the cottage on a rainy Fall day doing some editing of what was written, I came across a misspell by Nene and decided to focus on receptivity. I struck a chord when I decided to follow the prompt and explore the significance of receptivity in having a successful ADC.

When I received my training for IADC (induced after death communication), Cesar, the facilitator, commented that using the word induced implies that you are pushing or even forcing the experience. A successful IADC requires a quiet non-forceful receptivity to whom and what wants to show up.

As I reflected on this, the idea of induced labor popped into my mind. I know there are often medical reasons for inducing labor, but the action of forcing labor rather than waiting for the natural gestation process to unfold has a very artificial feel to it. Someone I know had a harrowing four-day ordeal in giving birth (ultimately Cesarean) after an induced labor actually before the due date. This, to me, seems to be the antithesis of receptivity.

Receptivity implies openness, waiting, trusting and patience. This is the "state of being" absolutely required to have a successful "After Death Connection." The image of a butterfly landing on a person's hand is a powerful metaphor for the energy of receptivity. No one has to be told that a butterfly could only land on a quiet, still, receptive person.

In writing this, I was aware of my tendency to move back and forth between pushing or forcing and allowing the words to come. I am sure this is an aspect of our humanity and certainly the way we are trained in our Western culture. This is a part of all of us.

After death communication, I believe, only occurs in a state of receptivity. That human part of us that wants to take action can be used in the service of developing the skills to create a state of receptivity within ourselves. In the service of offering these skills, here is another list from Nene on how to create a state of receptivity.

Nene's List of Skills to Create Receptivity

1. Sit down
2. Be quiet
3. Focus inward
4. Close your eyes
5. Breathe deeply
6. Remain focused

"Just as we learn lessons with classmates in school, our families play a similar role. They are our classmates in this school we call life."

Patrick Matthews

When you bring your
vibration to a certain
frequency, you tune to the
channel I'm able to
access you from.

Nenie Beanie

SHIFTING

When you are driving a car with a manual transmission, you can feel when you are in first gear or fifth gear. Nobody can explain the feeling to you. Once you become familiar with the car you have a feeling in your body and a knowing that tells you when you are in each gear and how and when to shift from one to another. Originally, you have to be taught by someone how to do it. You learn how to read a tachometer and that provides a guide as you are progressing in your learning. Eventually it becomes second nature and you become an expert at shifting from one gear to another and can identify which gear you are driving in by a felt sense in your body.

The same is true with dimensions. Quantum physics is teaching us that everything is energy and energy moves at different rates of speed. Some people call it vibration. How we experience our world is directly related to the vibration or speed of energy we are tuning into. We are like receptors. We tune into energy fields like radios tune into channels. If we want to listen to rock and roll, we tune into one station; if we are in the mood for classical, we change the station to another; if we are feeling mellow and we want some smooth jazz we choose that channel.

Choosing to tune into different dimensions is very similar to tuning a radio. The difference is we are the radio and the different dimensions are the different channels.

Just as we have to learn how to shift a car from one gear to another, and we know how to change channels on a radio, we can learn how to access some of the dimensions that our loved ones who have crossed over are residing in and communicate with us from.

How Do We Shift

*R*eligious and Spiritual teachings offer us many ways to shift dimensions.

1) Meditation is still the most common and effective method for moving to other dimensions, raising your vibration.

2) Moving oneself into an alert, present state of mind and connecting through writing is a most effective means of communicating with loved ones who have crossed over.

3) IADC, which stands for induced after death communication is a specific type of EMDR, It is a very effective way to create a communication with loved ones who have transitioned.

4) Dreaming is another state of consciousness, in which loved ones often make an appearance and deliver a message. This is called a visitation.

5) Many people are assisted in hearing from loved ones by mediums. These are people who are adept at accessing other dimensions through practice and use of natural gifts they are born with. Most mediums believe that we all have this ability but must actively develop it.

If you really want to connect with a loved one who has died, there are many ways to pursue this desire. As you tune into your own intuition, which are the ones that appeal to you the most?

Vibing

Almost everyone has heard phrases like "he has a weird vibe" or "she has a great vibe" or "we were on the same wave length." These statements are wonderful markers to help explain a fundamental aspect of ADC. You have to be on the same wavelength, on the same vibrational level.

Living in the material world, we tend to live in a certain frequency or vibration. Unfortunately, dominant in our mainstream culture is the energy of fear. Certain mindsets or emotions that are human include fear, anger, guilt, and grasping are not inherent in the vibrational field we inhabit when we are connecting with a loved one from the other side. In order to connect with them we have to be "vibing" or tuned in, or connected with the vibratory field they live in or as close as we can.

This vibration does not include these lower frequencies I described earlier like guilt, fear, grasping, To connect, we have to prepare ourselves by bringing ourselves onto the same wavelength, and finding a way to release the energies that prevent an ADC.

Techniques

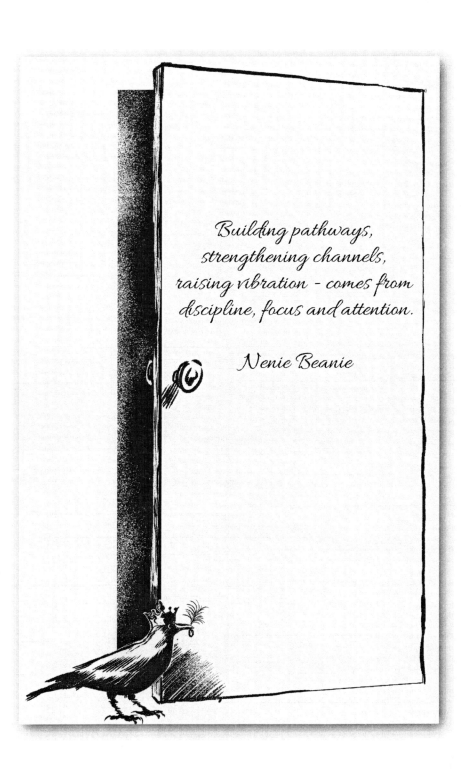

Building pathways,
strengthening channels,
raising vibration - comes from
discipline, focus and attention.

Nenie Beanie

Nene's List of Stops and Starts

In moving rapidly toward the completion of the book and being in awe of the unseen support I was receiving, I decided to deepen my connection with Nene and recommit to her as a co-author.

Her response was beyond my expectations, of course. As I was writing to her and listening intently to her response I received another "misspell." This time she wrote, "stop" twice as I was scribing what came through me from her, "As I've learned over the years I switched into an increased alertness and began opening up more attentively to what came.

Nene's favorite modality of conveying information was list making. So, again, she gave me another list. So, I took a deep breath, trusted, and wrote Nene's List at the top of the page. First, she said, "Relax, let go, flow with ease. These are the ways to be, "Stop with the struggle."

Then the list came; first came the stops.

1. Stop struggling
2. Stop predicting
3. Stop controlling
4. Stop efforting
5. Stop judging
6. Stop resisting

7. Stop denying
8. Stop distracting
9. Stop procrastinating

As I was dictating this list of nine behaviors to stop, I then began to receive their counterparts and began writing an accompanying list of "Starts."
Starts:

1. Start flowing
2. Start living in the moment
3. Start letting go
4. Start acting with ease
5. Start accepting
6. Start allowing
7. Start acknowledging
8. Start focusing
9. Start acting

Once completed this became "Nene's list of Stops and Starts." Upon reflection, I realized that this list is not only a wonderful way to live life, but it can powerfully support a successful IADC experience. Once contact is made, maintaining that connection would be powerfully supported by this amazing list of Nenes's Stops and Starts.

"Guided writing works beautifully because your hands are direct conduits to your heart – the place where your loved ones speak to you."

Sonia Choquette

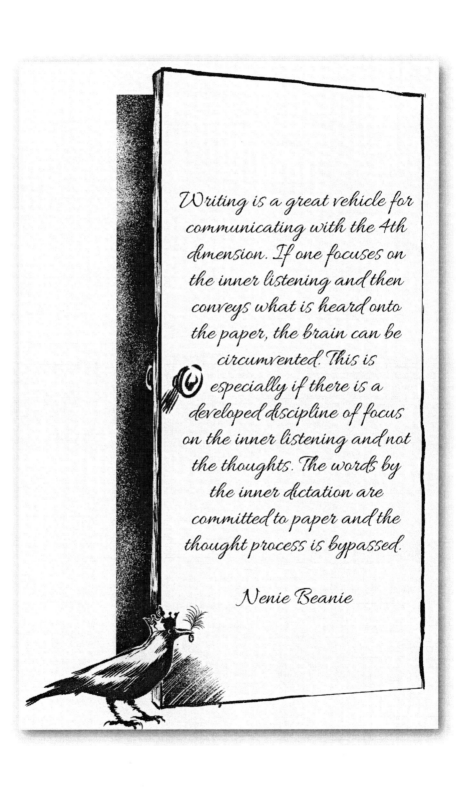

Writing is a great vehicle for communicating with the 4th dimension. If one focuses on the inner listening and then conveys what is heard onto the paper, the brain can be circumvented. This is especially if there is a developed discipline of focus on the inner listening and not the thoughts. The words by the inner dictation are committed to paper and the thought process is bypassed.

Nenie Beanie

LISTENING AND WRITING –A TECHNIQUE

1. Create a quiet space.
2. Focus inward.
3. Find location of inner ear.
4. Maintain focus there.
5. Ask self a question:

    Examples of questions:

    What am I here to do?

    What do I want to experience today?

    What questions do I want answered today?

6. Write the answer.
7. Write, also, one sentence or word about experience of inner listening.
8. Share experience with other

"Being Comes From Within."
Nevie Beavie

Writing as Meditation—A Practice

*Q*uieting the mind—releasing past and future—allowing the words to flow through the pen while observing your hand moving across the page. Relinquish judgment, listen intently internally and write the words that pop into your mind; trusting and honoring the silence. While waiting for the words to come, record them onto the paper, keep going by staying with the energy and allow the spaces—listen to the silence between the words and trust the process—letting it be. Do not force anything…allow…allow…allow.

You are creating a river of energy. You are moving into a lake of silence. Be in the lake. Float in the lake. Trust the process. Allow it to unfold naturally. Let it be without censorship. This is a practice in non-judgment. Judgment blocks the light. Feel the ocean of your body and allow it to be the way it is. Accept, allow and relax, writing whatever words come through.

This is a practice that creates altered states. It helps you shift dimensions. Judgment lowers vibration. Allowing, accepting raises vibration. Accelerated vibration shifts one's awareness into a higher dimension.

This meditation can be recorded and used to create a receptive state.

"... It means finding the invisible within the visible. You have a soul. And that's what the spiritual search is all about."

Annie Kagan
The Afterlife of Billy Fingers

Automatic Writing as Spiritual Practice

Questions for Loved Ones on the Other Side of the Veil

1. Who are you?
2. What do you want me to know?
3. What do you want to say?
4. How do I need to use my energy right now?
5. What do I need to know or do to love more?

*"When you ask for guidance, those in spir-
it will lead you in the right direction."*

Jeffrey Wand

Putting Pen to Paper

*P*utting pen to paper is a powerful vehicle for connecting with other dimensions. As you do this, you make a channel or a bridge that strengthens the more you practice it.

Here is how we do it!

1) Move into a centered place within yourself (your inner body)
2) Find your inner ear
3) Write what comes
4) Suspend judgment (crucial)
5) Maintain your focus on your inner ear and the pen on the paper.
6) Circumvent the brain.

The brain is to be used in service of the Spirit. Civilization has trained us to use it to negate Spirit.

The more you practice these things, the stronger your connection with Spirit will become.

Guaranteed –
Nenie Beanie

Enjoying The Fruits

God's big win is accurately
called heaven.
Heaven is God's victory
celebration. Not ours!
And the banner over the
eternal banquet will say
one thing.
"Love is stronger than death."

Richard Rohr

CELEBRATION

*A*s I was connecting with Nene this morning, I got a strong sense of celebration. Then as I began to write the word celebration, I experienced another misspell. That's always a sign from me that Nene has something important to say.

Earlier, I had picked up Sonia Coquette's book, *Ask Your Guides: Connecting with Your Divine Support System*; the page I read stressed trusting the experience of guidance. When a misspelling comes through from Ms. Right, I am getting better and better at trusting, actually experiencing, and knowing it is strong guidance.

Many of the reports of connection with the other side report that celebration is a primary energy that exists in the afterlife - Heaven. As we experience it (bring it here) we spiritualize matter, bring heaven to earth. As we access this high vibration energy, we can embody it in the creation of heaven on earth.

As I became clearer and experienced this energy, I wondered what the specific ways we could play our part to expand these energies on Earth. Celebration is an energy that enormously raises vibration.

As I wrote, a vision of an explosion of pink blossoms on a cherry tree in spring popped into my mind. This elicited thoughts about how nature celebrates. The woods by my house are blanketed in purple myrtle and white-trumpeted trillium early in May.

Moving more deeply into the energy I was experiencing these images conjured up memories of the song I had learned as a little girl, rehearsing for our May processions at St. Dominic Catholic Church. The hymn began with the words:

"Tis the month of our Mother
The Blessed and glorious days
When our lips and our spirits are glowing with love and with praise.
All hail to Dear Mary
The guardian of our way.
To the fairest of Queens
Be the fairest of seasons sweet May. "

As I write this, I am carried away with the energies of celebration and the example Mother Earth gives us of celebration, especially in the spring. Celebration invites the energy of Oneness. We gather together, we create beauty.

Beauty, Oneness and Joy all raise our vibration. Focusing on these higher qualities invites the energies of heaven onto the Earth plane. I am beginning to understand more clearly that celebration is an energy that invites heaven onto earth. With our celebrations, we can invite our loved ones who reside in heaven to not only celebrate with us but to bring their highly elevated celebratory energies into our celebrations with us.

In doing these, we progressively thin the veils between heaven and Earth and open the floodgates from Earth to heaven.

As I have my own experience in researching and writing this book, I am becoming progressively clearer that this "great uprising" or "opening the floodgates between heaven and Earth" is really the actual experience of bringing the energies of heaven to earth.

I see it in so many ways:

(1) The preponderance of books about connecting with heaven in the afterlife.

(2) The acceptance by the mainstream population of open conversation about experiences.

(3) The popularity of ghosts, ghost movies, TV shows.

We are really beginning to know that the energy we carry affects more than we can ever imagine. Celebration is an energy that connects heaven and earth.

When you ask for guidance
those in spirit will
lead you in the
right direction.

Jeffrey Wands

FINISHING

just read a section in a book about the fear of finishing or not finishing a book. I wonder how many accomplishments are lost through this fear. In writing to Nene this morning, she said, "If you channel me the quality of the work will be exponentially expanded."

So, now here I am writing exactly what is coming through without thinking or censoring.

What keeps popping into my mind is Marianne Williamson's famous quote "Our greatest fear is not that we are inadequate... our fear is that we are powerful beyond measure." Fears about finishing and not finishing (a double bind) prevent so much wonderfulness from being expressed and experienced in the world.

The *Course in Miracles* teaches that there are only two emotions, love and fear. It also teaches that love is stronger than fear. Beginning with enthusiasm, excitement, and beautiful intentions on a project such as writing a book is a wonderful thing. Being stopped or delayed by fear is tragic. So much is lost with giving up and shutting down.

Because this writing is a true collaboration with Nene, I turn to her and ask, "Where are we going with this?" As I do this, I feel a strong sense of Presence and recognize we are still connected even though I do not understand where we are going with this. She responds, "Just keep going, keep writing, and don't give up" and so I do.

Continuing to go forward when I do not know that where I am going requires drawing on the faith I have developed. The faith in my connection with Nene, so I continue on. I stop writing, tune in, and feel the connection. We are definitely on the same wavelength. Actually, the connection is continuing to strengthen as I listen more to her than my own head and my own doubt.

The energy is so strong now that the doubt is dissipating. I am finding myself so much more strongly immersed in the energy of my soul. She then shows up visually and says, "It is so important that you finish this book. The amount of love experienced, embodied, and acted from is beyond your wildest dreams. Keep going, finish it and release it to the world. Delaying is not an option. Do it, and do it now."

As I completed this writing I wondered was this only for me or also for the reader. What I realized is that as each of us connects with our loved ones on the other side of the door, the potential for the expression of so much more love on the planet is realized.

Potential is a wonderful thing, but actually moving to completion has benefit to us all and requires tremendous courage. Completing this book, for me, is an act of courage. I hope my efforts and intentions—and my truth— have value for you, as you read it.

Namaste

"In addition to being subtle, instead of speaking to us in direct language, spirits can use riddles, metaphors, symbols, dreams, and even jokes to speak to us."

Sonia Choquette

A Family Comes Together
Version Two

*T*his second story entitled "A Family Comes Together" conveys the impact of a mother who crossed to the other side 30 years earlier.

This experience catalyzed by a man's love for his mother that resided within a 40-year-old man who "lost" his mother when he was 11 years old. The healing that occurred within him as well as his two brothers and father was a result of a journey that began when he first realized that he had never adequately grieved the loss of his mother.

The events that unfolded were facilitated by his grieving process and a belief within him that his mother's spirit was still alive and deserved to be honored and acknowledged.

He requested that I include his story for the book and I was delighted to do so. I believe it is a demonstration that it is never too late for the healing power of love.

Throughout the process of writing this book, I maintained an active psychotherapy practice. Approximately a year into the research, I began seeing a John Smith (not his real name). He came to see me for stress related to the workplace. It became clear almost immediately that he was still being powerfully impacted by the death of his mother when he was a young boy.

As my client began discovering that he was still grieving his mother's death, he began to talk more about how his life changed when she died. He began to see how he had cut himself off from his feelings at this point in his life and started working with the memories of how he adapted to going on without her.

Spontaneously, he started visiting places in town that he remembered she loved. This led to his going to a special place in a local park and sitting. Although he had no dramatic connection with her, he continued to follow his own internal guidance system.

He placed four rocks the center of a clearing of ferns and came often to the park to connect with her at this place. After some time of doing this, he asked his father for some of his mother's ashes and spread them among the rocks. He showed this to his family and his wife suggested they erect a bench there in her honor.

His brothers became involved and offered to pay for the bench, which they acquired, and had a plaque inscribed for her. All three brothers and their father gathered to honor and connect with her spirit. This was a powerful experience for all.

In visiting his father weekly, he requested boxes of old family photos. Fortunately, they took many vacations together, usually spending time camping and hiking. These trips were well documented. He reviewed and scanned them and sent them to his two brothers on the other side of the county. He also shared them with his father who he visited weekly and viewed the photos with him on his father's television. . This took tremendous dedication, as there were several hundreds of them. In sessions each week, he would share the most significant photos he discovered and talk about them. Prior to this, his father had never spoken about his mother after she died.

He began regularly visiting the bench and special place he felt connected to her. In the meantime, he continued to scan and share photos of the family together before his mother left. He shared these with all of his family now including his two adult daughters who never met their grandmother. The family healing deepened and continued.

Inspired by this, one of the brother's wives created several magnificent coffee table books for the three brothers and father of many of the most special images. My client also began printing significant photographs and framing them.

All of this took place over a period of about three years. He sometimes commented that he never had a direct communication with her, but clearly his connection with her was deepened and his relationship with her was continuing with her spirit. He was not a religious man, but he came to trust himself and his experiences through this process.

He did say, however, that he did receive a vision of wise women in circle including his mother and a friend she had before she died. This was clear and powerful and occurred three times spontaneously in our sessions. It would be unlikely that this could be scientifically proven, but it certainly brings to mind, for me, Nene's last words, and "The circle of love is never broken."

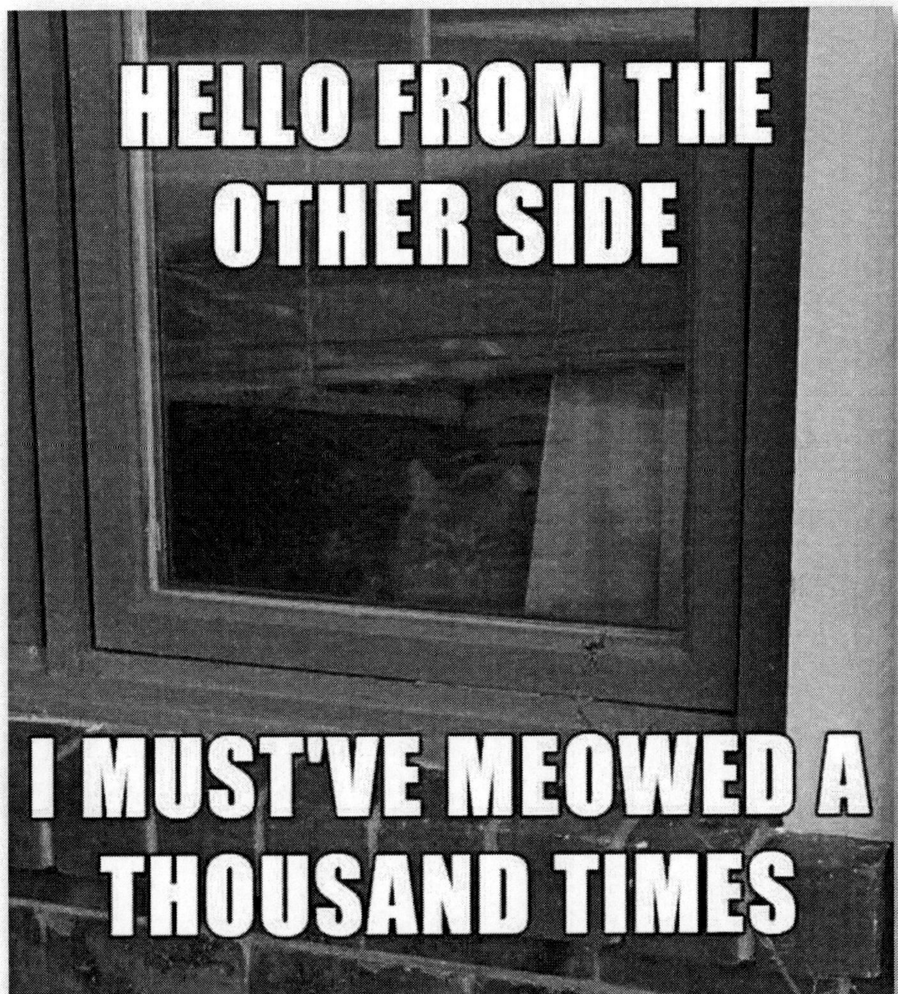
HELLO FROM THE
OTHER SIDE
I MUST'VE MEOWED A
THOUSAND TIMES

For the Fun of It

As I was nearing completion of this book, Nene's cat, Pumpkin, was diagnosed with kidney failure. The process of his dying was rapid and the vet and I were able to reduce his suffering by choosing to euthanize him at what was clearly the right time for him. I comforted myself by believing that he was now with Nene.

This is a meme that showed up on my Facebook timeline three days after he crossed over. The cat in the photo looks exactly like Pumpkin. The magic of this synchronicity reminds me of the fun and playfulness that is often a quality of spirit.

Playfulness and fun belong in this inter-dimensional connecting.

Pumpkin brought that message home to me.

Signs, Symbols and Connections